SAGGISTICA 15

Italy's Lies

Debunking History's Lies So That Italy Might Become A "Normal Country"

Lorenzo Del Boca

Translation from the Italian by
Ilaria Marra Rosiglioni

BORDIGHERA PRESS

Library of Congress Control Number: 2014948816

This book first appeared in Italian as

L'Italia bugiarda:
smascherare le menzogne della storia per diventare finalmente un Paese normale
Edizioni Piemme, 2013

Published by
BORDIGHERA PRESS
John D. Calandra Italian American Institute
25 West 43rd Street, 17th Floor
New York, NY 10036

SAGGISTICA 15
ISBN 978-1-59954-084-9

PUBLISHER'S NOTE

We wish to thank Lorenzo Del Boca for his second volume with Bordighera Press. Such an occasion to publish his work in English helps create a greater dialogue between Italy and the United States. In this same vein, we also need to thank Vincenzo Marra, president and co-founder of ILICA (Italian Language and Inter-Cultural Alliance) for his vision of the necessity of such a dialogue. Ilaria Marra Rosiglioni, in turn, has been our most able and dependable translator in this and other books that Bordighera Press has published in collaboration with ILICA.

This is the latest in a series of volumes we have published with ILICA. As we have done in previous volumes, we have followed a more American style in the book's production. However, with regard to the bibliography, we decided to keep the actual texts that the author originally cited in his Italian edition, even if they were translations from another language, including English.

Rebecca Rizzo provided indispensable assistance during the production phase of the book, with her keen eyes for editing and proofing. In a similar manner, Professor Stanislao Pugliese offered his editorial advice during his reading of preliminary proofs.

A tutti, un caloroso grazie!

Fred L. Gardaphè
Paolo A. Giordano
Anthony Julian Tamburri
FOUNDERS, BORDIGHERA PRESS

TABLE OF CONTENTS

PREFACE

The history books recounting the origins of many countries are filled with lies. There is not one single nation that can boast a history of its foundation that is completely truthful. Patriotism is also composed of a legendary aspect that includes stories that have been tweaked or sweetened. How many omissions were made in recounting the myths surrounding the French Revolution? How many fabrications have been made, including the Scottish kilt which symbolizes the Scottish identity when in reality, this article of clothing was introduced to Scotland at a much later time. Perhaps it is all inevitable. Perhaps we cannot do without an element that binds a community together and that fashions history as though it were an epic tale. The actions taken by those orthodox censors, those high priests professing official truths, those guardians of the correct representation of the past that has been authenticated by the State's seal of approval are all bothersome. They are impatient and intolerant. All they seem to do is launch excommunications and anathemas. They have exercised their powers against Lorenzo Del Boca as well. For many years he has craftily undertaken the task of challenging dogmas and vulgates, which has led him to be considered enemy number one amongst the writers of the sacred history of the unified State. How does Del Boca dare to question the moving, epic history of the House of Savoy? Is he challenging the spirit of our unified country?

No. In the pages of this book Del Boca yet again demonstrates that he is not nostalgic for the past. He is not a backwards secessionist. He does not intend to sabotage the country. He is not paid by the "Enemy" to be a provocateur. He is a curious and irreverent journalist. When he sniffs out a lie perpetuated by the State, he grabs his pen (or his computer) and decides to dismantle it, dissect it, and reduce it to pieces. He reconstitutes the profile, not of an alternative Truth (we are laypeople, not clergymen against clergymen), but one that is a bit more turbulent and speckled, decidedly less triumphant. Del Boca puts his journalistic skills at the disposal of a new and less catechistic historical investigation. He offers his flair for detail, his suspicion of the protagonists' sincerity when they speak of their own actions, his ability to catch contradictions, and his ability to navigate amongst the shadows of what is left unsaid and what remains unclear. Being the purebred reporter he is, and I am qualified to consider him as such as I have had the great fortune of working and collaborating with him in the offices of the newspaper *La Stampa*, he hunts for documents, fragments, and any clues that might demonstrate the presence or even suspicion of an "official" lie. This is why his books, this one especially, are filled with data, elements upon which we are called to reflect. One might not be in agreement with Del Boca's complex theories, but one cannot but appreciate his precious efforts to dig up the truth, his constant challenge to the laziness posed by "official" truths and those who perpetuate the Great Lie. Italy always seems to slip on the hypocrisy of small and big lies that deform the sense of its national events. How many "non-truths" about the Risorgimento, WWI, Fascism, the Resistance, the Republic, and all the way through to the Second Republic and its never-ending agony, tend to multiply and generate new ones that are always cloaked in bad faith. Their penchant for being tampered with has no rival amongst any other modern nation. This is why the works of someone like Del Boca are even more indispensable in Italy than elsewhere: to dismantle some lies, to restore some luster and faith in the value of research, to destroy some fragment of the Lie. We need this.

Pierluigi Battista

Italy's Lies

Debunking History's Lies So That Italy Might
Become A "Normal Country"

ONE NATION, INVISIBLE, AMIDST THE CHURCH STEEPLES

For the 150th Anniversary, Turin, and here the truth must be told, flew the tricolor flag of Italian unification with the enthusiasm akin to its status as the kingdom's ancient capital. For the merchants present in the city's historic center, perhaps it was even in their best interest to do so in order to please the tourists that flocked there. Certainly, those merchants located outside of the city center had no real reason to fly the flag from their balconies other than to effectively celebrate the event and to secure bragging rights for their nationalistic pride. However, in the other regions of the country, it seems to me as though the various events planned to remember the anniversary of Italy's Unification fell under the seal of approval of a bureaucracy that did what was expected. At times, they seemed even annoyed to plan such events.

As a sort of "wake-up call" to his readers, Massimo Gramellini summarized such a sentiment of disaffection towards a celebration as reminding him of "those birthday parties thrown for adolescents where at the last minute the invited guests either bail out of going or drag themselves to go by the force of inertia and with the secret desire to stir up some trouble." He goes on to recount: "We managed to lose the President of the Province of Alto Adige, who feels more like an Austrian abroad." Then, "the president of the industries, a magnanimous soul, on that day she is ready to uncork a bottle of sparkling wine, but at the workplace: no vacation day because in the global economy, it is more important to increase the GDP rather than one's belly." According to Gramellini, forty days prior to the event, many Italians ignored the real reason for the festivities, or did not care, or even used the occurrence of the anniversary as a pretext for dividing Italy all over again. The Pro-

Bourbon advocates would very much like to drag the Piedmontese before the court at The Hague. The residents of the Padania region are divided among those who consider Cavour a victim of Garibaldi or his accomplice. "But underneath it all, everyone is convinced that we have been united by a historical accident to which we must succumb but that is not worth boasting about."[1]

Come to think of it, "Fratelli d'Italia": what brothers? The nation came to be as the result of fraud, subterfuges, ambushes, and reprisals. Should the victims of these actions actually be satisfied with having been swindled? Should they sing the praises of those who cheated them?

One hundred and fifty years ago, at the dawn of those movements that would bring about Italy's Unification, Italy seemed to be a patchwork quilt, divided as it was into a large quantity of states and regions that impeded its development. The North was divided into the Piedmontese State in the West and the Lombardy-Venice State in the East. The Center was divided into the Vatican State, the Duchies of Modena, Parma, Piacenza and Guastalla, the Grand Duchy of Tuscany, and the Republic of San Marino. The South was ruled under the Kingdom of the Two Sicilies. Each State had its own currency that was not even remotely related to that of its neighbor. Only Turin employed a decimal system that required the use of multiples of a different consistency.[2] The country was truly composed of "patches."

Every trip, no matter how long or short, was an adventure. One had to consider borders, customs taxes as well as different laws and administrative systems that were quite different from one another.

A simplification was absolutely necessary. The merchant world, in some fashion, was already devising a change of its own accord. It employed the use of Turkish piasters as the token of exchange. In modern terms, as a means of comparison, it is equivalent to today's use of the dollar.

---

[1] M. Gramellini, "È qui la festa" in *La Stampa*, February 8, 2011.
[2] R. Bracalini, *L'Italia prima dell'unità (1815-1860)* (Milan, 2001).

Forget about the romantic dreams of an Italy that was ideologically united. These were merely the visions of poets. The initial projects to "fix" the nation regarded establishing a customs "league" that would allow for easier travel and that would facilitate tax payment for those products in circulation.

Economic problems were dealt with prior to addressing the political issues at hand.

The plan was to establish a federation that functioned in a manner similar to the administration board of a company in which each locally elected government would, proportionately, hold a certain amount of shares. Who would be the President? It might very well be the Pope-King. Vincenzo Gioberti imagined that, through the authority attributed by *moral suasion*, this sort of "golden share" could be given to the Pope.[3] However, not everyone was in agreement. Antonio Rosmini, though a priest, was attracted of the idea proposed by the Swiss whereby the President could be anyone amongst the representatives of the various Cantons.[4] It seemed to him as though assuring a consistent change in the government would guarantee the collective nature of the board and the equality of each of the federation's members. Nothing, however, was done.

In order to reach a satisfying result, it was necessary to employ a great deal of mediations in order to address all of the issues, large and small, that everyone raised. It was necessary to find solutions that would please everyone.

Camillo Benso, Count of Cavour, had the stature and the intelligence to face such a daunting task and to come out victorious. However, he preferred to take a shortcut, first relying on assistance provided by France and England and then manipulating Giuseppe Garibaldi's tan-

---

[3] M. Sancipriano, *Vincenzo Gioberti, progetti etico-politici nel Risorgimento* (Rome, 1997).
[4] C. Riva, *Missione diplomatica di Antonio Rosmini a Roma* 1848-1849 (Rome, 1966).

trums to unify the country with arms. He took the quickest way out, without taking too many precautions, keeping his eye on the objective.[5]

Meanwhile, in those same years, merely a few hundred kilometers away, Otto von Bismarck was engaging in numerous discussions in order to unite the German *Länders* under one flag.[6] The "weaver" of our nation called forth all of those who supported his plans and sent them to battle and shoot those who had different ideas.

The two projects were similar but had two drastically different outcomes. In the North, Prussia was established: the "grandmother" of Germany, and the engine of Europe. In the South, Italy was established, though despite some literary efforts, only on paper.

This is because the Unification of Italy, the day after its establishment, was no longer liked even by those who made the effort to form it.

The South, ferocious and rebellious, was brought to its knees by 40 battalions of soldiers that considered those provinces to be lands of conquest. Naples and Palermo were not treated differently than, decades later, Mogadishu and Addis Abeba. They said they came to bring freedom, but they showed the freedom they brought through the crosshairs of their rifles and the tips of their sabers.[7] Those who refused to defend their independence were considered "brigands."[8] Their economy was destroyed and they were burdened with taxes. They were made to starve and those who did not emigrate wound up, in large numbers, in front of the firing squad. Their liberator "brothers" were those who shot the very "brothers" they had freed.[9]

Even after 150 years, in the absence of an honest reinterpretation of those events, is it possible to forget everything, pretend nothing hap-

---

[5] D. Mack Smith, *Cavour, il grande tessitore dell'unità d'Italia* (Milan, 1985).

[6] A.J.P. Taylor, *Bismarck* (Bari, 2004).

[7] L. Del Boca, *Maledetti Savoia!* (Casale Monferrato, 1998).

[8] A. Nicoletta, *"E furon detti briganti," Mito e realtà della conquista del Sud* (Rimini, 2001).

[9] P. Aprile, *Terroni. Tutto quello che è stato fatto perché gli italiani del Sud diventassero meridionali* (Milan, 2010).

pened, fly the tricolor flag as per the request of President Carlo Azeglio Ciampi and President Giorgio Napolitano?

The Church was on the war path until the accord signed with Benito Mussolini. With the justification, which truthfully was hypocritical and demagogical, that the State needed to occupy itself with the body and the priests needed to worry about the soul, the patriots of the Risorgimento stole as much from the Church as was possible. In accordance with the Law of Siccardi, they confiscated lands, convents, ecclesiastical goods, and small treasures that the locals had bestowed upon their patron saints. For the record, the confiscated wealth could have covered the national debt, but only a small amount ever actually reached the State Treasury. Only a few swindlers managed to increase their wealth by buying pieces of land as big as provinces for mere pocket change.[10]

In 1859, the patriots of the Unification managed to take the region of Emilia Romagna from the Pope. In 1860, with the excuse of defending him, they managed to take Umbria and the Marche regions. Finally, in 1870, they forced open the gate of Porta Pia with cannons and seized the region of Lazio and the city of Rome, thus relegating the Pope to Vatican City. For a half-century, the Catholics considered the Risorgimento to be an abuse of power towards the Church and refused to participate in political matters. They proclaimed, "We are neither electors nor the elected," as though they were exiled in their own State. Since then, the majority of Catholics have overlooked this and made peace with the reality of the situation, but not quite all of them.[11]

Even in the North, one must ask, "What unity?" In Modena when the insurrections, called for by Cavour, ousted Duke Francis V Habsburg-Este, the Duke's army followed him into exile. They were 584 men who were led by Alberto Saccozzi that, in an orderly fashion, left the city

---

[10] A. Pelliccari, *L'altro Risorgimento, una guerra di religione dimenticata* (Casale Monferrato, 2000).
[11] A. Socci, *La dittatura anticattolica. Il caso don Bosco e l'altra faccia del Risorgimento* (Milan, 2004).

and followed their leader into exile.[12] They did this to illustrate the point that they believed what had happened was dishonest. If this was the new Italy, then it was no good. Many efforts over the years were made to prompt the soldiers to return but no one accepted the terms offered by the Italian government, even when the Duke was forced to discharge them because he was no longer able to pay them the minimum wage.[13]

What Italy? Not even the old region of Lombardy-Venice where the mythical Five Day Insurrection took place to prompt the beginning of the Unification process, seemed satisfied with the way things were going. The first to complain were the very patriots that, in the line of fire, had given the greatest contribution to the liberation of that region.

"These were not the agreements made... you had agreed to undertake different tasks...": It is with these words that Gabrio Casati, from Milan, who was named Minister of Instruction in order to give the government more credibility, gave his letter of resignation by throwing it forcibly upon a table.[14] They were in too much of a hurry to implement Piedmontese statutes and to establish Piedmontese institutions in Lombardy. The initial hypothesis was to gradually fuse the two regions together, taking the best that each had to offer, in order to reach a union that was not only acceptable to both but that could actually be of some merit as well.

Many studies were conducted and many projects were laid forth. A commission was established and presided over by Count Cesare Giulini della Porta, also from Milan. He had a patriotic pedigree that was respectable, having participated in the provisory government established following the Five Day Insurrection in 1848. Only Lombard citizens were called to elaborate the definitive documents, and they did so without any local prejudices. It is for this reason that the fruit of their labor was considered "interesting." Their interpretation of the sociopolitical

---

[12] E. Bianchini Braglia, *In esilio con il Duca. La storia esemplare della brigata Estense* (Rimini, 2007).

[13] Ibid.

[14] D. Mack Smith, *Cavour.*

scheme of the newly established State delineated what should be done to incorporate the new provinces. The present administrations were to be held in consideration because many functioned quite efficiently.

Respecting the local governments and encouraging them to better themselves, as protagonists, seemed to be the right recipe for obtaining significant, and practical, results. Even in Turin, the intellectual elite were in agreement. A study conducted in the previous year, in 1858, compiled by Teodoro di Santa Rosa, saw the expansion of Piedmont in the same light and proposed identical solutions.

The government (or perhaps we should be more specific and mention only Rattazzi) in theory approved the suggestions laid out by those documents and declared that it planned to operate on the same wavelength as the notions stated. In practice, however, it behaved as though it did not take any of the suggestions into consideration. Rather, the government behaved much more like an overlord that has the power of decision and proceeded to enforce its decisions.

"The agreements made, on the basis of which we shared the burdens of war, are not being respected...."

Rattazzi decided to extend the penal and civil codes to include the region of Lombardy. He managed to pass those laws that allowed for (and in some cases obliged) the State's interference in provincial and municipal governments. He promulgated regulations regarding education with contents that can be considered far more centralistic than the present-day Boncompagni Law.[15] These regulations were destined to remain in vigor well into the following century and even then they were only retouched during the Fascist regime through the Gentile Reform.

The Lombards felt betrayed. They were not considered to be equals and they were not even considered to be capable of carrying out the least of the administrative tasks. For each new administrative position that opened up, a Piedmontese was sent to fill it. Sometimes the choice of

---

[15] C. Cantù, *Della indipendenza italiana* (Turin, 1872-1877).

personnel proved inadequate and the "new" director wound up causing friction.

It was impossible not to complain about the administration that took the place of the Austrian one, which was efficient by definition. The Savoy substitute, while still testing the waters, managed to be inconclusive and was not capable of meeting the needs of the people.

Telegrams took around 10 days to reach their destination and, in February of 1861, the salaries of the previous month had not yet been paid. Was all of this revolution carried out to substitute Vienna with Turin? Were the Habsburgs sent away merely to put the Savoys in power?

The newspaper *La Perseveranza* concluded: "Each of our observations is met with a reproach: you are local governments, you are Lombards, and you are youths that are merely threatened by the specter of Piedmontism. We complain of the disorder present in public offices; the loss of certain institutions that were at one time florid due to their experience; the hasty application of laws that are unnecessary. How do they respond? You are Lombards and your politicians are too provincial."[16] According to the newspaper, it was impossible to contest that the recent positions filled were merely decided upon by Piedmontese recommendation and not by an open public selection. It was prohibited to highlight the mistake made by transferring the headquarters of the Lombard railways to Turin. It was pointless, and in some cases dangerous, to state that a French instructor's qualifications could only be established in the city of Turin.

Il Pungolo, a sharp-tongued daily newspaper released in the afternoon, wanted to highlight the incongruencies in the latest justice reforms: "Turin laid its hands on the system and promptly disconnected it. It has altered the entire economy and, may we add, has done so thoughtlessly!"[17]

The Lombards wound up alienating themselves and managed to become the critics of the country. This attitude greatly irritated Piedmont.

---

[16] *La Perseveranza*, February 22, 1861.
[17] *Il Pungolo*, March 11, 1861.

Turin constantly complained that each time they had to make a decision they found themselves having to deal with a tiny slice of society that complained and criticized their every move.

But, in the end, the Unification of Italy did not seem to please even the Piedmontese, who had made many moral compromises to ensure that it took place. Costanza d'Azeglio wrote (to summarize the general sentiment) to her son Emanuele: "No one here wants to join with Naples for reasons that only a Piedmontese could comprehend." The Southerners seemed to be people that were too "distant." Rather, they believed such a union to be dangerous and akin to "mating with a corpse."[18] It remains to be understood, if Piedmont truly entertained these opinions and prejudices, why the Piedmontese did not just stay home, much to the satisfaction of nearly the rest of Italy.

Was it over? In 1866, the third war of independence occurred, in which Italy partook, thus taking advantage of the conflict between Prussia and Austria, our historic enemy. Truthfully, Vienna, in order to not be fighting a war on two fronts (in the North and South), would have been inclined to leave us the Veneto region. However, the government, along with Victor Emanuel II and his empty-headed military commanders, deemed it to be dishonorable to merely be given a territory.

We needed to conquer this territory through battle! In this manner, we sacrificed the lives of many soldiers and national honor. They destroyed us in Custoza, on land, and in Lissa, by sea. They beat us two to zero with no mercy.

In Lissa, in the heart of the Adriatic Sea, Viennese ships were captained by Venetian sailors that, when they fired shots at the Italian fleet, shouted either "Leon...!" or "San Marco...,"[19] depending on whether the crew hailed from the city of Venice or one of its provinces. They won the battle, against any prediction. Their commander, Admiral Tegetthoff,

---

[18] M. Costa Cardol, *Ingovernabili da Torino. I tormentati esordi dell'unità d'Italia* (Milan, 1989).

[19] E. Beggiato, *Lissa, l'ultima vittoria della Serenissima (20 luglio 1866)* (Rimini, 2012).

proclaimed how "men of iron, on wooden ships had the better over heads of wood aboard iron ships." The "wooden head" with the most experience was Admiral Carlo Pellion di Persano. Hailing from a town near Vercelli, he was used to the water in the rice fields, which is never too deep and he was unaccustomed to the waves of the sea. He did not know how to swim and insisted that he be accompanied by two robust sailors who could rescue him in case he risked drowning. Once he returned to his port he had the gall to proclaim victory.[20] He immediately participated in the festivities that instantly ensued. It was only after a few hours that he had to face the dire news.

Those soldiers that had fought and won on Austria's side, the following day, due to an international treaty that had ignored their presence, found themselves to be a part of the Kingdom of Italy. They used to pay 11 lira in tax money that went to Vienna and within a span of 18 months, those taxes increased to 32 lira that they were forced to send to Rome. The "passante di Mestre" the portion of the A4 highway that bypasses Venice, was only recently built. Could they really be supporters of the Unification?

And what of those soldiers from Trentino who, during WWI (1915-1918) fought in the trenches of the Karst Plateau for the other side, found out at the end of the conflict that they needed to change their uniforms? It had been decided a few weeks prior, in London, that Italy would no longer be neutral in favor of the Triple Entente with a treaty that had been signed by England and France.[21] Obviously, these two countries did not bother to consult those citizens that were directly affected by this agreement! With how much fervor do we really think that these people should wave the tricolor flag?

There is no "Unified" Italy because it simply does not exist. The nation's true roots are not planted firmly in the Risorgimento but rather the

---

[20] A. Lumbroso, *Il processo dell'ammiraglio Persano con una prefazione e un'appendice di documenti inediti sulla campagna navale di Lissa (1866)* (Turin, 1905).
[21] L. Del Boca, *Grande guerra, piccoli generali. Una cronaca feroce della prima guerra mondiale* (Turin, 2007).

Renaissance. The country matured under the rule of Lordships and townships. This happened in a time when its attention was focused on the confines of its local parishes: it was this element that defined our identities.

It is not rare to find that still today neighboring towns, even of the same province, maintain a very cordial disdain for each other. At one time this disdain was cause for war and alliances were made with faraway towns in order to defeat one's neighbors. Today, some of the ancient chants and jeers still remain along with some cultural gaps that are difficult to fill.

"Those from Pisa cannot stand to see Lucca" is the esthetic metaphor for those bits of society that were built around their local parish church. "The Venetians are great lords, the Paduans are great professors, those from Vicenza eat cats, and those from Verona are completely insane," is a verse from a popular chant.

The Bourbon rulers, up until the nineteenth century, had chosen Naples as their capital, but theirs was the Kingdom of the Two Sicilies. The sovereigns ruled from beneath the Vesuvius, but could not do anything to make that historic island their own. It was not even considered to be one Sicily... it was two! One belonged to the Sicilians and the other to the Sicans, the latter of which came from a faraway place and though they learned to live together they still maintained their own customs and a certain distance from one another.[22] Francis and Ferdinand appointed a viceroy to Palermo, who had a great deal of power. This served to acknowledge and formally grant that acceptable level of freedom that his subjects claimed.

The other districts in the kingdom were the Calabrias and the Puglias, and they are referred in the plural as if to confirm that there is no ancestry between the Ionic and Tyrrhenian coasts. This is similar to the separate worlds, and at times antagonistic attitudes, portrayed by Catanzaro and Reggio of Bari and Lecce.

---

[22] M. Spataro, *I primi secessionisti: separatismo in Sicilia 1866 e 1943-46* (Naples, 2001).

Piedmont, perhaps because it is stuck between Switzerland and France, or maybe because under Savoy rule its government resembled a military base, seemed to be the most compact region.

Yet there are at least three discernible Piedmonts.

The provinces of Novara and Vercelli are Lombard. The people there speak a dialect that has a cadence similar to that of Milan's. The economy was shaped by Ludovico Sforza, Duke of Milan. In order to protect his city from malaria, he ordered the rice fields be moved by twenty leagues, effectively transplanting them to the surroundings of Novara and Vercelli.[23]

To the right of the Po River lies Savoy-ruled Piedmont. The region was centered on Turin and its dialect was reminiscent of the French language. In fact, the French influence could be detected in its style and its culture.

About 80 or so kilometers further South, towards the Apennine mountains, one comes across a cluster of towns: Novi Ligure, Rocchetta, Ligure, Albera Ligure, and Mongiardino Ligure. The "Ligure" at the end of each of their names might lead you to think that they belong to the province of Genoa, but actually they are within the confines of the province of Alessandria,[24] though this would seem to be by pure chance. The spoken dialect is drawn out, as can be heard in the songs by Bruno Lauzi and Gino Paoli. In the outskirts, the people use the Ligurian measuring stick, which is a bit shorter than the Piedmontese one. Those who buy land must pay attention to avoid paying for 10,000 square meters and winding up with only 9,500. These conditions allow for the Piedmontese purists to dictate their ideal confines along the banks of the Tanaro River, to the South of which lies the rest of the world.

All of these specifics, in certain instances they are quite extraordinary, cannot lie under one sole blanket, even if it is tinted with Italy's three colors. There is no common denominator. We cannot find one and

---

[23] M. Frigeni, *Ludovico il Moro, un gentiluomo in nero* (Milan, 1980).
[24] G. Redoano Coppede, *L'archivio storico di Novi Ligure. Appunti per una storica della città* (Rome, 1989).

to impose it would mean recurring to the violence of a dictatorship. Let us not even think of such things....

This "parish" mentality paints a picture of an Italy that is rife with antagonism and that is argumentative. It is close-minded and egotistical. In other words, this offers a negative image. In the past, it has happened that we refused to accept progress because it might benefit our neighbor as well.

All of this individualism, however, can offer something positive. Each community offers an abundance of advantages and goods that can only be considered as an added value. Each town, even the smallest and most remotely located, has a heritage that is rich in art, architecture, and even culinary arts that when summed together and adequately promulgated is certainly worth a few more GDP points.

Part I

Impossible Reforms

CHAPTER 1

THE CONSTITUTION? SCRAP METAL

What about the Constitution? Well, yes. It really is the equivalent of scrap metal.

I understand that, in choosing this way of stating my opinion, in a context of euphoric rhetoric that is filling all of the pages of our printed media, I run the risk of proposing a sort of parody of the *Fantozzi* movies and of his much celebrated exclamation regarding the *Battleship Potemkin* movie.[1]

This definition, if it does not appear entirely unrefined, could seem hurried. Yet, even though one risks oversimplifying the concept, it is perhaps better to speak clearly and therefore avoid one of the main defects of our country's culture of speech. Often, the speaker presents his or her argument by saying certain things and alluding to others, piquing curiosity, in order to declare, though only in part, something. The other part must, however, contain some sort of retraction of the previous part. It is as though one were to propose a thesis with a built-in refutation of its inherent concept.

Therefore, the Italian constitution, with its 65 years of activity, should seek a well-earned retirement as it would in any country at any latitude in the world. The truth is that it could really do with retirement, despite the unfavorable legislation regulating social security that, everywhere is an accomplice to an improvement in lifestyle, manages to keep pushing back the day of its final bonus paycheck.

---

[1] *Translator's note*: He makes a rather lewd, but humorous scatological remark regarding this acclaimed film.

With all due respect to those who preoccupy themselves with proclaiming articles as though they were Bible verses, considered to be "far-sighted" and in some instances even "prophetic," the fundamental basis for the laws of the State are comparable to an old man riddled with ailments, who drags himself along with the help of his crutches trying not to lose his balance, but always on the brink of being pushed to the ground and trampled by the crowd that is in a hurry and has no time to worry about an old man and his illnesses.

The Constitution's supporters, though they may be motivated by notions that are ideally irreproachable and even commendable, should really just give up. By defending it, they are causing the paralysis of this country, burdening it with unnecessary baggage. They are adding lead weights to its wings and hindering the possibility of making decisions after-tomorrow (in other words late). Decisions that should have been made the day before yesterday (in other words in their due time).

This piece of paper that is the foundation of a country, in order to function properly, should limit itself to delineating a few definitive principles of general order which would define its ideological confines.

Can I cite an example? After the French Revolution in 1789, the French chose their historic three word motto: "*liberté, égalité, fraternité.*" Their constitution was voted upon on September 12, 1791. It was composed of 7 "titles," of which the third was divided into 5 "chapters."[2] Its lexicon was understandable, despite the fact that it was a document that broke with the traditions of the past and required expressing concepts that had not ever been put into practice because they had been forbidden by the previously used political jargon.

The United States, which was more pragmatic, chose to orient itself towards the "pursuit of happiness." Since they chose to immediately address the heart of the matter, they limited themselves to 7 articles. Obviously when changes became necessary, Congress made those modifications. At the moment, there are 27 amendments and they are each ap-

----

[2] A. Mathiez, *La rivoluzione francese* (Turin, 1970).

proximately only one line long. For example, the 13th Amendment abolishes slavery and the 15th confers upon those former slaves the right to vote. The 19th Amendment gave women the right to vote and the 27th, with extraordinary intuition, limited salary increases for the members of Congress.[3]

England actually manages to do without a State Constitution. It does not exist. This is in spite of the fact that in that very place in 1215 the *Magna Charta* was drawn, and it is the "mother" of all of the constitutions of the free world. When one refers to "The English Constitution," one is actually referring to a volume published by Walter Bagehot in 1867. Thanks to the initiatives proposed by Il Mulino publishers, it is now also available in Italian.[4] For the Parliament in London, the laws are all equal: there is no need to establish a hierarchy, whereby some laws are less important than others, and are therefore subject to them.

As far as Italy is concerned, it decided to declare itself to be "democratic and founded on the basis of labor" operating under the "sovereignty of the people." The eleven articles that follow the first would have been sufficient.

Are they concepts that are excessively generic? Perhaps.

Do they border Utopia? Certainly.

Equality and brotherhood have not yet obtained citizenship in Paris, or in other cities of the planet for that matter, but it is still appropriate to recall them in making one's plans. Even though happiness may not have been obtained in the United States as of yet, it must still remain an object of pursuit. Just as the "sovereignty of the people," though we may be far from practicing this concept, it is still an objective that must be pursued with even greater vigor.

The Italian Constitution, rather than distinguish between values that would be indispensable to focusing on future prospects, together with the 12 articles that we could define as "principles" tacked on another 127,

---

[3] A. Testi, *La formazione degli Stati Uniti* (Bologna, 2003).
[4] W. Bagehot, *La Costituzione inglese* (Bologna, 1995).

making the total 139. This is 40% more than the constitutions of the rest of Western Civilization. No matter which way you turn it, we lose in any comparison. Even the old Russian Constitution of 1917 seems simpler. Since we are speaking of the work of Leninist Comunists in the attempt to define, in detail, who had the right to vote and how they were to exercise this right in the *kolkhoz*[5], it is quite paradoxical.

In our Constitution, there are also the basic elements for numerous ongoing debates amongst the various institutions of the State.

For example: Article 127 states that, "the Government, when it retains that a regional law exceeds the competence of the Region... can question its constitutional legitimacy.... The Region, when it retains that a law or an act decreed by the State or by another region oversteps its sphere of competence can question its constitutional legitimacy...." Those who are well-versed in such matters specify that this is called "concurrent legislation." Basically, it comes down to being a paradise for those who love to argue. It is a field day for lawyers who amass trial after trial in which there are always two "constitutionalists" present. These are always university professors of constitutional law, each of which takes a side to debate the legitimacy of the matter at hand. This only goes to prove that the Constitution allows for at least two interpretations.

The Constitution also has numerous duplicate and triplicate laws whose applications span the infinite. These often manage to revoke responsibilities towards those who should be held responsible and acting as an obstacle to the implementation of necessary amendments in a timely fashion.

It all appears as though it were an enormous cart that moves in slow-motion, with the parking break pulled.

An example of how gummed up this system is would be the concept of "perfect bicameralism." This is the basis under which a bill (even an important one) could bounce around back and forth between the branch-

---

[5] R. Pipes, *La rivoluzione russa* (Milan, 1995).

es of the government for years without ever going beyond the mere level of inconclusive chitchat.

Months of debate amongst the various commissions (first) and in the various chambers (second) are necessary in order to examine in detail the text of the legislative measure.[6]

When and if this measure has the great fortune of attaining the definitive vote, the approved document, along with all of the papers it has accumulated along the way, is transferred to the other branch of the Parliament where the whole process begins again. This is not out of distrust towards their colleagues, but rather out of respect for their own role in the government.

So the approval of the measure begins once again, from the ground upwards. The investigations begin once again and the same analyses are consulted once again from the beginning. The experts that were previously consulted once again return and new experts are proposed. At the end of all of this work and all of these verifications, could one really accept the measure without so much as adding a comma to modify it? This is sufficient to send the entire file back to the beginning once again: in fact, the Constitution states that the two branches of Parliament must approve a law that has identical texts.

Perfect bicameralism often means "tricameralism" and "quadricameralism"...or even penta[7]...

Could a company, any company, in any part of the world survive in the market with two directors of personnel, two marketing offices, two chains of distribution, two buyers, and two accountants?

How could Italy ever hope to survive?

To be honest, the Constitution managed to add a few additional complications for good measure.

Once a piece of legislation passes through the Parliament, the file that has been discussed (and fought over) for numerous months by depu-

---

[6] S. Baldelli, *W Montecitorio! Guida pratica ai misteri dell'aula della Camera* (Soveria Mannelli, 2012).
[7] Ibid.

ties, senators, counselors, experts, secretaries, and consultants is actually still not a law. The file must reach the Quirinale hill and reach the President's desk where he or she must verify if the text is compatible with the fundamental principles of Italian Law.

If the President's answer is negative and he or she does not sign this bill, it once again returns to square one and the examination and whole process begins again.[8]

If the President signs the bill, it still is not a law! The bureaucratic procedure is still not over.

The Constitutional Court or the State Council could still block the entire procedure by finding some error in form or some contradiction. For example, they could discover that in laying out a certain law, the Council of Ministers overstepped their own authority, thereby annulling several tons of papers that have been painstakingly compiled. Everything must once again return to the beginning!

In order for a law to pass, 600 acts (with relative signatures) must take place. When procedures are flowing smoothly, it is not surprising that there is no government.[9]

I understand that what I am saying might come off as irreverent, but this is all very similar to the Game of the Goose, even though this is all hardly a game. Every time one casts the dice one risks finding oneself at the beginning of the game. It is not entirely up to chance. But certainly chance and luck are unpredictable factors that are undoubtedly present. In this case, the times employed along with the manner and procedures, which are fundamental for any country, represent the greatest unknown factor. This renders our system extremely fragile. Is it appropriate to defend it to the point of becoming its staunch supporters?

---

[8] Ibid.
[9] Ibid.

CHAPTER 2

A GOVERNMENT WITH TWO PRESIDENTS

An example of perfect bicameralism: the Prime Minister and the President of the Republic are actually duplicates of the same role whose responsibilities overlap, causing confusion.

The ancient Romans, after ridding themselves of Tarquin the Proud, imagined that the best course of action was to place the Republic in the hands of not one, but two men. They believed that one man alone could foster hegemonic tendencies and preferred to employ to consuls who would act as each other's guard dogs. The risk that the two men could waste their time creating obstacles for each other was overcome by appointing one in charge of international affairs and the other in charge of internal affairs.

The consul who was given the task of handling international affairs had to defend the borders and territorial conquests. He lived at the edge of the empire, thousands of miles away from the capital. He was all about muscles and action and wore armor. He fought against the enemy and ruled over his soldiers with an iron fist.

His colleague, the consul in charge of internal affairs, lived in Rome and took care of all matters pertaining to public order, regulation of commerce, food supplies, and in general the correct functioning of the entire administrative apparatus. He was generally calmer than his counterpart and took care not to make hasty decisions. He needed to ensure that life in the capital and its provinces proceeded in the manner deemed fit by the Senate.[10]

---

[10] M. Rostovtzeff, *Storia del mondo antico* (Florence, 1965).

The Prime Minister and the President of the Republic today both live in Rome, but 2000 years later. The distinction between their powers is lost. For some time, they represent a parallel diarchy with one headquarters in the Chigi Palace and the other at the Quirinale Palace. They are approximately 600 meters apart from one another and they both stir the same pot with similar results.

Are two institutional figures with analogous duties necessary?

Around the world, consolidated democracies have established that one figure is more than sufficient. The people vote and choose the person that will govern their country. The person who obtains the most votes has the task of building a team they feel could help them most in accomplishing the tasks set forth in his or her electoral program.

In several states, such as the United States, France, and Russia, one president is elected who assumes complete responsibility for the executive branch. There is either no Prime Minister, or he or she is nominated by the President to whom he or she must report.

In other countries, such as Germany, Greece, and Portugal, a Prime Minister represents the executive branch while the president assumes a role with a lower profile. For example, in Berlin, *Frau* Merkel is the prevalent figure while most people do not even know who the President is. We might remember that at the beginning of 2012 he was involved in a scandal that called for his resignation.[11] But one must do more research before stumbling upon the name Christian Wulff. The same goes for his replacement, Joachim Gauck.[12]

In Spain, England, Holland, and Sweden, there is still a monarchy and the king or queen in power represents the unified country. Their duties however, only extend far enough to include a speech given once a year, without participating in any political matters. They are distinct and distant.

---

[11] G. Russo, "Christian Wulff si è dimesso" in *International Business Times*, February 17, 2012.
[12] A. Tarquini, "Un pastore protestante è il più anziano dei presidenti della Germania" in *la Repubblica*, March 18, 2012.

Even in Italy, for about 40 years or so, the Presidents of the Republic limited themselves to their end of year speech. Either from the radio (when that was the only means possible) or from a television channel (when television came to broadcast more than one channel) the head of the State spoke to the citizens in a tone of voice similar to that of a wise grandfather. He offered a report on the past 12 months and wished everyone the best for the next 12. In the beginning, only a few minutes were sufficient to offer a message of good luck. Over time the President's Speech on New Year's Day went on to become a true report of all the country's positive and negative sides. It was not very concrete and became wordier and at times downright boring. In spite of this, the following day's comments involve praising the President's sagacity.

For the rest, his or her life is composed of routine public appearances and a secluded political life. This became sort of a self-imposed limitation, as though the President wanted to renounce taking on certain roles and making decisions that they felt exceeded their sphere of influence.

The revolution began with Sandro Pertini, who took to making public appearances around Italy regularly. Pertini was exuberant in both his ways and in his character. He enjoyed being with the people and never missed an occasion to do so. He requested to be taken to a field in the town of Vermicino, half way between Rome and Frascati, where a young boy, Alfredino Rampi fell down a well. He wanted to take part in the rescue efforts and encourage the men who were trying to help the boy. He wanted to show his solidarity. Their interventions, however, were futile. The child died and Pertini cried. He cried real tears.

His frequent appearances came from the heart and from his desire to participate.[13]

His successors embraced political matters as well. Francesco Cossiga became known as the "Pickaxe Man." This is because through his use of words he highlighted problems and issues along with things that needed to be done and measures that no longer worked. "Pickeaxe Man" was

---

[13] C. Angelini, *In viaggio con Pertini* (Milan, 1985).

actually a moniker coined by Cossiga himself when on March 23, 1991 he decided that he would no longer hold back from speaking his mind. He considered his vitriolic declarations to be merely "statements."

"I delivered such blows to the system with my pickaxe skills that it can no longer be restored. It must be changed."[14] Argumentative by nature, he resigned two months before the end of his mandate and expected to be called President "Emeritus." He did not like the prefix "ex" and did not want it used to cite those positions to which he had been assigned.[15]

Francesco Cossiga freed political language[16] from its hypocritical and repetitive formulas. His way of speaking resonated amongst the youths of the time.

Oscar Luigi Scalfaro, who succeeded Cossiga when the First Republic was collapsing on itself under the weight of numerous investigations, aside from one instance of personal disappointment, resumed the same type of rhetoric employed during the Fascist period.[17]

His period was a complex one, during the course of which he did not hesitate to let his voice be heard, at the cost of facing an avalanche of criticism tied to his decisions. Lodovico Festa, in his book *Ascesa & declino della seconda Repubblica* went as far as calling him the "Boogeyman."[18]

He blocked Amato and Ciampi, who were both busy trying to find a political solution to come out of the *"Mani Pulite"* scandal. He accepted the diktat of the Public Prosecutor of Milan Borrelli. He allowed for the "martyrdom" of Andreotti. He assisted the incredible "preventive persecution" of Berlusconi because he chose to enter politics. He imposed his veto when the lawyer Previti was nominated to the Ministry of Justice by stating: "That name shall not pass on my desk."[19]

---

[14] P. Guzzanti, *Cossiga uomo solo* (Milan, 1991).
[15] Ibid.
[16] V. Sgarbi, "La rivoluzione della "boiata" in *Il Giornale*, June 20, 2012.
[17] Ibid.
[18] L. Festa, *Ascesa & declino della seconda Repubblica* (Rome, 2012).
[19] M. Breda, "Da notaio del Parlamento al "non ci sto" in *Corriere della Sera*, January 30, 2012.

He dissolved the two Chambers in 1994 without seeking any outside council and in 1995 he appointed Lamberto Dini as the Prime Minister when Berlusconi's first administration found itself in the middle of a crisis.

Berlusconi, from the very beginning, accused Scalfaro of having cheated him because he had initially promised to call for an election when in fact he called for a provisory government. He also made sure that this government lasted as long as possible allowing the opposing party to fortify itself.

Respectable experts stated that a similar eruption had never before occurred in political history. This is something that would not normally be stated by an institution which considers itself above and beyond partisanship. The involvement of the Head of the State was both personal and direct. This was revealed by Umberto Bossi on September 8, 1996 in response to Scalfaro's position against the Lega party's pseudo-secessionist threats. Bossi declared that in December of 1994, he and the President made a secret pact to ensure the collapse of the Berlusconi government. Following this agreement, under the auspices and advice of Scalfaro himself, the Lega party broke from the Forza Italia party, who held the majority vote, and became the opposition. Basically, this was an underground *coup d'etat* that was conceived and nurtured within the walls of the Quirinale Palace.[20]

There was nothing truly certifiable in his actions. They were the determined and resolute initiatives taken by a leader who developed and carried out his program. *The Economist* wrote that "Mister Scalfaro was not a bad president but he became convinced that the Italians needed to be treated like children, with a Nanny-President." The question that the magazine posed was "Does Italy need a Nanny-President?[21]"

Even the Presidency of Giorgio Napolitano has been characterized by its constant, direct, and resolute involvement. He managed to deter-

---

[20] R. Scarpa, *Scalfaro* (Rome, 1999).
[21] J. Hooper, "La presidenza di mister Scalfaro" in *The Economist*, March 26, 1990.

mine certain critical elements of politics by his direct actions to the point where the provisory government of Mario Monti was dubbed the "President's Government."[22]

Paolo Granzotto, in his column in the *Il Giornale* newspaper responded to a letter written by Gaetano Rodolfi, noted how the First Lady went to vote for the primaries of the Democratic Party. "She could have made due without the photographers and cameramen accompanying her to the voting booth. I certainly hope that she will not come back and tell us that it would have been difficult to accomplish." This might seem to be a detail of secondary importance but it serves to underline the idea that the President of the Republic handles matters personally. "Being the wife of the Head of the State requires that certain measures be taken. For example, one must adapt to the role of the Head of State's spouse. According to the Constitution, the nature of this role lies in representing all Italians."[23]

The journalist Mario Cervi, speaking of Napolitano, concludes with a generally positive opinion. Yet he too must honestly admit that "there are those who cannot stand him and evoke his past as a Communist by accusing him of subversive scheming."[24]

To return to the point: in Italy the Prime Minister and the President of the Republic are two personalities that operate in a parallel fashion to one another. They mirror each other's actions and have powers that cross over, collide, and impede one another.

Is this a paradox? A Prime Minister wins an election but in order to fulfill his elected role he must be officially "appointed" by the President of the Republic. The Prime Minister chooses his governing team of individual ministers, but these ministers in turn must swear loyalty to the country at the hand of the President of the Republic. When faced with

---

[22] E. Mauro, "Il Governo del Presidente" in *la Repubblica*, November 14, 2011.

[23] P. Granzotto, "La first lady non è al di sopra di ogni sospetto" *Il Giornale*, November 29, 2012.

[24] M. Cervi, "Il 2012? Poteva andare peggio: ci siamo salvati dalla fine del mondo" *Gente*, January 3, 2013.

great difficulty, it is not the government who decides to throw in the towel and call for an election. Nope. The Chambers are dissolved by the President of the Republic who, amongst his many prerogatives, can determine the beginning and end of a given legislature even if the people (the essence of a democracy) have already clearly expressed their wishes.

One can object by saying that for the past fifty years or so the various governments were born out of a series of coalitions established after the elections and amongst parties that initially seemed unwilling to cooperate. The voters often had no idea who would obtain the majority in Parliament.

It was only with Berlusconi that it immediately became apparent who had won: then came Prodi, then came Berlusconi again, then Prodi again, then Berlusconi....

This, however, serves to bolster the case made by those who believe that constitutions are the products of their historic and sociological contexts. If those contexts and social conditions change, then so must the constitutions.

The structure that surrounds the President has grown exponentially in light of the President's increasing appointments at the Quirinale Palace and his trips in Italy as well as abroad.

Since he must take care of internal and foreign affairs, handling the relations with the Holy See along with managing legislation, justice and the armed forces he requires a staff of 2,181 people. One must also include the 16 forest rangers at the President's estate of Castelporziano.[25]

In San Rossore there was also once a herd of dromedaries. Ferdinando de' Medici brought them there since he loved all things exotic. The animals bred and the already numerous herd had already increased in size when a large quantity of camels joined them from the Turkish army that had been defeated at Vienna's gates. The herd survived through monarchies, the Unification of Italy, and made it to see the Republic. Some wound up in circuses while many were devoured by the "Mongolian"

---

[25] R. Costa, *L'Italia dei privilegi* (Milan, 2003).

Mamelukes that were enrolled in the *Wehrmarcht*. After September 8, 1943, they were given a space on the estate in which they could set up their camps. Then President of the Republic Giovanni Gronchi attempted to revive what was left of the herd but they refused to procreate and the herd completely vanished.[26] This story is a curious one, but it is incomplete. Nowhere was it ever recorded how much this herd cost the Italian people to maintain.

The Quirinale has become a "bonsai" government with counselors that in reality act as sort of "mini-ministers" or shadow ministers.[27] I use the term "bonsai" loosely because it is an institution that is both gigantic and omnivorous.

During the presidency of Luigi Einaudi, the journalist Indro Montanelli, who was at the Quirinale Palace conducting an interview, was invited to stay for lunch. At the end of the meal, the President, with an apple in his hand, offered him a piece: "Would you like half?"[28]

These were times of austerity.

Now, the budget of the President of the Republic reaches around 235 million euro, including the 250,000 euro of his salary. In comparison to all the other expenses, the President's salary is one of the smaller ones. The economic crisis however managed to encourage some measure of austerity. Starting from 2008, the budget was reduced by 1 million euro. In other words the budget was reduced by 0.53%.

Just for comparison's sake: the Queen of England manages to survive with a staff of 300 people and a budget that is six times less than that of the Quirinale Palace. The King of Spain employs 543 people in his staff and his budget is eight times less. The White House employs 466 people and costs one third of the Quirinale's budget. The Emperor of Japan, who is of divine descent along with his entire family, squeaks by with a court of 1,000 people.

---

[26] P. Granzotto, "Nell'"Angolo" si parla di utile e di futile. A patto che sia dilettevole" in *Il Giornale*, June 6, 2012.

[27] M. Cervi, "Ma quanta costa il Quirinale?" in *Il Giornale*, January 30, 2007.

[28] M. Campiverdi and F. Ricciardi, *I menù del Quirinale* (Milan, 2011).

Can a country like ours still afford a Quirinale Palace that is so lav-ishly exuberant?

It seems as though the President of the Italian Republic, in order to guarantee the nation's unity, has an impartial role that comprises that he must also preside over the Supreme Council of Defense and the Supreme Council of Magistrates (which is the institution that regulates the entire judicial branch). But if the President (as has happened) finds himself contending with the Public Prosecutor (of Palermo) and, even if against his will, in litigation with a party that he should be representing, then his impartial role goes out the window. It simply does not exist.

CHAPTER 3

THE CONFLICT:
NAPOLITANO V. ATTORNEY GENERAL OF PALERMO

It is the very conflict that developed between President Giorgio Napolitano and the Public Prosecutor of Palermo that, with our Constitution, it is unlikely that we will make much headway. In the little progress
we might make, we will constantly encounter obstacles in our path.

In order to better comprehend the matter at hand, which is actually
quite complex, a few premises must be made along with a mention of a
few historic episodes. These will allow us to reconstruct the context of
the investigation conducted by the magistrate.

A group of Sicilian magistrates, coordinated by the Public Prosecutor
of Palermo Antonio Ingroia, began to collaborate to sort out a complex
series of events that occurred between government officials and prominent members of the Mafia. These events began during the *stagione delle
bombe* (bomb season) between 1992 and 1993. It was at this time that the
Mafia used bombs to destroy the Georgofili Institute in Florence, the
colonnade of Saint John in Lateran in Rome, and that ultimately took
the life of Giovanni Falcone, who up until that point had been fighting
the Mafia with significant results.

Organized crime launched a frontal attack on the State in order to
blackmail it and oblige it to come to their terms. As paradoxical as it
might seem, this aggressive attack managed to obtain its goal because
these government officials immediately sought out these Mafia bosses
and an agreement was reached.

There is no irrefutable proof. There are no direct witnesses and
therefore the entire episode is based on a series of tentative details. How-

ever, when these details are put together they allow for a relatively clear picture to emerge.

Certainly, Florence's Court of Assizes gave this story some credit. The judges condemned about fifteen or so Mafia bosses for the massacre that occurred at the Georgofili Institute. The motivation for the sentence used 100 out of its 150 pages to explain the reason that inspired the attack. Their opening statement was quite inflammatory: "There is no doubt that an agreement was made and called for an exchange of favors. The initiative, however, was taken by government officials and not the Mafia bosses."

So what was bargained? The Mafia wanted to save 532 members of organized crime clans from jail. Article 41 of the Constitution was to be applied to these people. Nicolò Amato was the Director of Prisons at that time and he had already prepared the appropriate decrees that were required to jail these criminals. The decrees only required the signatures of the Ministers of Justice and Internal Affairs but this did not happen for many years.

The notion of a secret agreement is highly disturbing because it traces a clear connection between the State and the most combative branch of organized crime: this is the very entity that the State should be fighting, without "ifs, ands, or buts." If this hypothesis is true, then it is inevitable but to conclude that the highest government officials were involved. This is the first premise.

The magistrates from Palermo began their investigation and came upon a series of recordings of various telephone conversations. One of these phone calls concerned Nicola Mancino, former Minister of Internal Affairs and former Vice President of the Supreme Council of the Magistrate. Rather than become too alarmed, Mancino was disturbed by the investigation that concerned him and contacted the President of the Republic. He spoke with the Head of the State's judicial councilor, Loris D'Ambrosio, but at least a few times during the phone conversation, the voice of the President Giorgio Napolitano can be heard as well. Granted, the conversations were of little importance: they were calls made out of common courtesy. However, Big Brother's ear had violated the Quirinale Palace's privacy.

The entire issue came to light quite by accident following a few journalistic indiscretions that initially were more secretive and eventually became more explicit. These indiscretions referred to phone-taps conducted on illustrious members of the government to which the Public Prosecutor's office of Palermo had access. This is the second premise.

President Giorgio Napolitano raised this issue before the Constitutional Court, stating that the Head of the State cannot have his phones tapped and that if this were to accidentally occur, then the recorded conversations should be immediately destroyed.

The Public Prosecutor defended himself by stating that he acted in a correct and scrupulous manner.

The two theses, which are irreconcilable and opposing, were supported by two constitutionalists. They are scholars and experts of the Constitution that while it may be the most beautiful one in the world it is also certainly not the most easily interpreted one.

Professor Michele Dipace proclaimed "the principle of the freedom of the President of the Republic's conversations." This is obviously a constitutional dogma.

On the other side, Professor Alessandro Pace expressed his idea by *reductio ad absurdum*: "If one were to discover through a recorded phone conversation that the President of the Republic was planning a *coup d'état*, should the Public Prosecutor destroy that conversation?"

The Constitutional Court sided with the President of the Republic. It still remains to be understood why the Head of the State must be protected an iron-clad guarantee while the Prime Minister can be investigated even beyond the bedroom.

The decision caused a great stir. Antonio Di Pietro assured all that he would have done his best to present a draft law that would "bridge this legislative gap" that this issue made quite evident.

According to Antonio Ingroia, "the sentence had already been written for political reasons more than for judicial reasons." He added that, according to the Constitutional Court, "We should have offered a more creative interpretation of the law, which would have resulted in its being in violation of the law. If we had done what the court asked, in other words sending the judge the telephone recordings requesting their destruction, the judge would have ordered the Public Prosecution to file the charges and opened the case to cross-examination of the interested parties. Inevitably, these recordings would have been made public."

The case gained notoriety in July 2012. The Court took 80 days to decide if it would go to trial. It managed to express itself on December 4th. It took another month and a half to provide its judicial review.

This took a long time because the Constitution is contorted, murky, and widely contested.

The Constitution was approved by Assembly on December 22, 1947 and was promulgated on the 27th by the provisory Head of State, Enrico De Nicola. The document was then published in the *Gazzetta Ufficiale* and went into effect on January 1, 1948.

Do not let the closeness of those dates fool you.

The procedure by which it assumed its final form was a tiring and tortuous one. Of the 600 "constituents" it was necessary to appoint a committee of 75 people. Even this committee of 75 people, however, was further subdivided into a half-dozen other subcommittees to edit "this" or "that" part of the document or "this" or "that" article. Those who coordinated the effort modeled the system after that of a river and its tributaries and distributed different tasks to different committees while mainly occupying themselves with gathering the necessary information once the drafts were edited. Much effort was placed in executing this task and it is not a matter of criticizing either the level of competence or dedication applied, but the result was a tangled mess that barely managed to hold together the ideological and cultural notions it expressed because they were often incompatible. The texts that emerged from the subcommittees rose to the committee of 75 people and ultimately to the assembly as a whole. They were disjointed and derived from sources that were in discordance with one another. This conclusion was drawn by Piero

Calamandrei, a jurist who cannot be suspected of being prejudiced: "When we finally assemble these pieces that come from different, tiny offices, we may notice that the gears and cogs do not quite line up and that the joints that should hold the motor together do not correspond."

It is from this hybrid, if you are so inclined to define it as such, or if you prefer, from this confusion, that the Italian Constitution was born. According to many, it is a true legal masterpiece.

It is said that those who elaborated the texts operated with the notion, or obsession, of avoiding a new dictatorship in mind. The twenty preceding years, under the power of Mussolini and Fascism, had a severe impact on national politics. The Italians were terrified by the idea of despotism that had laid them into submission for too long. They felt frightened by any type of authority to the point that they chose to exorcise any elements that might ensure a dictatorship's return.

While this all may be true, the so-called "fathers of our country," or at least the wisest ones, more than the fear of the past, worried for the future. This group was a varied one: a little less than half were Communists of the PCI Party while the other half was composed of the Democratic Christians of the DC Party. The remainder was comprised of a few deputies from the Partito d'Azione, a few liberals, some Social Democrats, and a couple of Demo-Proletarians. These were well-educated people that were trustworthy and credible on a personal level. Some of them were even willing to tolerate the vestiges of a monarchy but they had no electoral following. They were destined to act as the "spare tire" of the larger more important political parties. Amongst these, the Communist Party openly supported Moscow, the Soviet Union, and the dictatorship of the Proletariat while the DC Party did everything in its power to ensure that this did not take place in Italy. They fought to maintain Italy in the Western bloc under the moral jurisdiction and protection of the United States of America.

It is quite evident how the Communists and the Democratic Christians played a game where they both contemporaneously participated as both allies and adversaries. They both collaborated and boycotted one another and pretended to help each other while actually creating obstacles for their opponents. Often, they blatantly lied, while being fully aware of their lying.

So who was their role model? Penelope: at night she unraveled all that she had woven during the day.

Even their behavior was like that of Penelope. She, with silence and discretion, lived in the dwelling that Homer defined as "supernal and fitting of a widow." She had but a few faithful handmaids that were capable of tiptoeing around the apartments as though they were ghosts. In a similar fashion, the politicians following the war used the hallways of the government buildings for prudent plotting. It was all plotting to put together projects that were in direct contrast to those of their adversaries. They were all well-orchestrated shams that were composed to disorient and subsequently sidetrack their opponents. These maneuvers were designed so as to allow their adversaries to believe that they had understood precisely the opposite of what was intended and to be free to act according to their own agendas. This was all done in a very mild manner: even sighs were perceived as a manifestation of an enthusiasm that was no longer in style.

This is all noteworthy to highlight the everyday state of politics that is not in any condition to get anything accomplished. The little that manages to get done, however, is promoted to death. The moment a politician comes up with an idea, he does not let one opportunity to recount it to any nearby journalists who pass by. Said journalists will of course dedicate the front page of their newspapers to make such an announcement.

In the worst-case scenario, one could resort to using social networks and a similar result is obtained. From there, the media circus begins along with a sea of declarations, contestations, approvals, and corrections that are all made of nothing and serve to add to nothing.

Politicians inform the public (who are also voters) of what they eat, what time they go to sleep, whom they salute on the street, where they plan on going on vacation, who their tailor is, and the titles of the books they plan to read over their summer vacation. Their behavior perhaps depends on the general "mood" of the government.

Even the members of the provisory government headed by Monti, as soon as they were in office, learned to deal with gossip concerning them and how to become protagonists.

The privacy laws are only enforced in cases when some piece of information that is obviously not in the politician's best interest is divulged.

Back then, information was handled with a completely different style. One proceeded with a caution that bordered on secrecy. On one hand, the KGB intervened with rubles from the Kremlin in order to finance Communist electoral campaigns while on the other hand the CIA tried to even the playing field with American dollars. There were few indiscretions and one could say that even those who were most informed did not have all the facts either.

Therefore, everyone was in agreement that it was important to ensure that Fascism did not make a comeback, though this was highly improbable. However, everyone was careful to subtract any power from one's adversaries so as to reciprocally prevent one another from gaining any ground in government institutions. Any effort made by either party had to be conditioned, prevented, thwarted, or at the very least slowed down to the point where it became necessary to reach an agreement.

The word "consultation" came into the lexicon a bit later but it was put into practice with the Republic.

With the Constitution, the Fathers of Our Country made great efforts to establish an institutional framework that was completely fractionated as though it were an enormous puzzle. Each piece needed to fit perfectly and therefore needed to be compatible with all of the pieces that bordered it.

The tiny particles of power were meant to be managed by a system of checks and balances and therefore had to be slightly compromised. Each piece needed to be worth something, but not much. The little power it wielded needed to depend on another piece whose power was conditioned by a third piece.

The moral of the story: whoever won, even if they did proclaim victory, could never avoid having to form some kind of agreement with those who had lost.

This entire structure is not immediately comprehensible and at times comes as the result of an elaborate web of connections: so-and-so nominates someone as the Head of the State, the Supreme Court must handle that other person, yet another person may come from the Parliament but in order to make any decisions a two-thirds majority is required. Any way a situation is configured, the Parties must arrive at an agreement. Shall we complicate things further?

The members of the college do not have terms that expire at the same time, so the renewal of their positions happens on different dates. The result is that the alleged majority party is actually in a precarious position. Its majority status is always unstable and therefore the leading party is always a little paralyzed.

In order to avoid either the PCI or DC Party (both parties were in ideological opposition and the times were violent ones) prevailing with absolute certainty, they found a way to mutually neutralize one another.

This was done most likely without their even realizing it: they both decided on a sort of programmed halt and settled for obliging one another to stop, or at least obliging them to take as little action as possible.

The easiest technique to halt any sort of progress would consist in posing obstacles to even the simplest government operations: calling for two Chambers when one would suffice, requiring two votes when only one was necessary, requiring two approvals instead of one, calling for two resolutions rather than just one... just double everything....

Chapter 4

One Job and Two Salaries

The idea of "2 for 1" became popular in supermarkets when they began to offer two products for the price of one. This invention came from the United States and found suitable terrain upon which to operate thanks to their favorable economy. To housewives, this idea was a fabulous one because it gave them the impression that they were saving money and allowed them to be a bit more generous in the kitchen.

Yet this product of American marketing genius was not invented in the United States. The notion of "2 for 1" had already been present in Italy for quite some time. The Italian Republic retains the "copyright" concerning the fact that for each office held the tasks are divided.

The only variation to the "2 for 1" idea consists in the fact that in this case, one can hold a job that pays two salaries. Sometimes it is possible that one salary might suffice to cover the problem, but it often happens that such "problems" remain unresolved and it is necessary to seek more assistance. In this case, a second office may be opened and a third salary may be necessary.

An enlightening example of how this technique is employed can be found in the case of a teacher from Verona, Giorgia Nani. In 1993, she was placed on a short-term contract at the city's elementary school. When she realized that she was pregnant, she filed to receive her maternity check. She first turned to the INPS,[29] but after a few weeks, they replied that they were not responsible for handling her request. The teacher then filed her request to the superintendency for local education,

---

[29] INPS is an abbreviation for "Istituto Nazionale della Previdenza Sociale," Italy's social security agency.

but even here, after many solicitations, the request was denied with the same response: they were not responsible for handling this type of request. Her only option was to turn to the Administrative Court, who took her request very seriously and left no stone unturned in finding an answer for this teacher's request. The magistrate interviewed everyone in question (and I do mean everyone!) and after 5,238 days, or approximately 19 years, reached the conclusion that Giorgia Nani was right and deserved to be compensated.

A similar case in any other part of the world would have been resolved with a simple telephone call in 1993. Can we refuse to assist a pregnant woman? No! Then the administration must be responsible for handling her compensation. The only issue to be decided is which office would handle the payment. In the end, it would not have mattered anyway since the funds would always have been State funds anyway.

In 1993, the teacher would have been entitled to a sum that amounted to slightly less than 10 million lira. Today, she is entitled to 5,089 euro. The difference in actual buying power between that amount then and now isn't even comparable and Giorgia Nani is bracing herself to bring a case against the State for the excessive duration of the trial and expects an adequate compensation. What remains difficult to calculate is the amount of paperwork that was involved in this case: correspondence between the administrative offices of half the country, involving a great amount of employees, lawyers, and magistrates...

Even in this instance, in any other part of the world those two employees that declared that their offices were "not responsible" for handling this woman's request would have been called by their respective directors and fired for being "irresponsible." Probably, in other parts of the world they would have asked that the State be held accountable for such a long trial. The sheer length of the trial and the sentence issued only served to render the country more ridiculous in the world's eyes. It is truly worth a place in the Guinness Book of World Records, albeit a negative one. In Italy, however, this would be impossible. This is because everyone defends him/herself by calling upon statutes and regulations that, unfortunately, reveal that they are in fact right. How can a country expect to move forward if there are so many rules that allow and authorize processes that both logic and common sense refuse? Or worse ... inspire snickering!

Everything is doubly complex. Everything is muddy and murky and nothing is done to shorten these procedures.

This has all become such a habit that we no longer even notice that we are accommodating this way of thinking. In the capitals of the provinces, matters of law and order are the domain of the prefect and the police commissioner. These two officers meet on an almost daily basis along with other influential members of the law enforcement team to coordinate operations. The fact that these meetings must occur so frequently means that each officer's tasks are not as well defined as one might hope. If each officer's tasks were so clearly defined, then why waste time reiterating what should already is well known? Certainly if there are so many officers traversing a gray area then perhaps it is best to clear the air in order to avoid stepping on the wrong toes.

A while ago, the Lega Nord Party began one of its "campaigns" to do away with prefects. They did not think that prefects were necessary because they were considered a symbol of a centralized State: in other words they were perceived as a bureaucratic presence that was capable of suffocating and weighing down the vivacious nature of the regional populations. This initiative was soon abandoned and never mentioned again. In truth, it was not even an original idea. Before Umberto Bossi, the President of the Republic Luigi Einaudi published an article under his own name with the title: "Doing Away with the Prefects." This served to illustrate that the country's unity was not determined by prefects, local departments of education, financial experts, municipal secretaries, or memorandums and instructions issued by the authorities in Rome. "Unity," he stated, "is determined by the Italians... that they might learn at their own expense how to govern themselves."

Prefects should be abolished, not because they represent the authority of Rome, Milan, or Turin, but because they are merely duplicates (or triplicates) of other existing authorities. Speaking of the spending review, aside from their salaries, they have at their disposal a vice prefect, a vice vice prefect and a slew of other staff members. They often live in a historic building that requires air conditioning in the summer and heat in the winter. They are escorted with a car that is equipped with a driver. They manage a budget that handles celebrations for June 2nd and April 25th. They require compensation for travel in order to reach Rome on the occasion of (often useless) general government meetings.

Our law enforcement systems are duplicates in nature as well. Italy is the only country in the world that has both Police and *Carabinieri*. Each one believes themselves to be extraordinary and perceive themselves to be singularly exceptional, though somehow they always manage to, absurdly enough, compete with one another. We should be the safest country in the world and yet we are the ones who manage to waste the largest number of forces as well as resources.

The same thing that occurs on the outskirts occurs in the cities as well.

Another vestige that should be classified as "scrap metal" is the diplomatic network that represents absolute stagnation. It is not a coincidence that to refer to this category, we journalists refer to them as the *feluche*, which were the hats that they used to wear in the nineteenth century.

That was two centuries ago.

For them, it seems as though time has stopped just short of the *Belle Epoque* when ambassadors caressed their feather pens while dipping them in their inkwells as they gave a careful daily account of the political events of the country in which they were living to the Minister of Foreign Affairs.

These reports were highly detailed and may have even contained some gossip here and there. They were an attempt at imagining possible developments with the caveat that they never tip the balance in favor of one side more than the other and to therefore never exclude the possibility of a strategic retreat. But today, with news that travels in real time, we must ask ourselves whether we really need this enormous staff of employees whose sole task is to inform us of what we can already know?

Among the personnel at the Ambassador's disposal, there is a counselor for economic problems. This is an appointment that could be extremely useful, but perhaps it is not enough. In fact, holding true to the logic of duplicate offices, in the majority of the cities where there is an embassy, or the more important consulates, there is also a Chamber of Commerce that should favor the import-export efforts of Italian companies. However, even this is insufficient. Usually a few hundred meters away, at the most, in the same neighborhood as this office, is also the ICE: the National Institute for Foreign Commerce. Its statute states that its duty is to facilitate economic contacts between companies but specifically with partners outside of Italy's borders.

Now, there is no doubt that scattered throughout the five continents among the thousands of employees that are working to promote and sell the "Made In Italy" brand there are many that are equipped, skilled, careful, worthy, and useful individuals that justify their salaries. But how many others step on each other's toes? How many entertain the idea that in the midst of all that chaos it is truly pointless to do anything? How many employees find it all too convenient to hide in the folds of hierarchical chaos even when their collaboration might be necessary?

The ambassador also calls for a cultural counselor. Wherever there is an embassy there is also an Institute of Culture, and its duties vary from city to city. One is situated in a historic building that is discrete and in the Rococò style, another inhabits the entire 14th floor of building H, and yet another is located in the same neighborhood as the European Parliament. The majority of them are operated by career diplomats who have participated in a selection process from which their diplomatic careers began. A few positions are reserved for appointment by the government, which fills them with worthy individuals,[30] though often their worth is

---

[30] *Editors' note*: The Italian expression is "per chiara fama," literally, "by clear fame", which better translates "by virtue of impeccable repute," or "distinguished."

apparent only to those who have nominated them. Nearby, we also have the Dante Alighieri Society whose sole aim is to promote the Italian language and culture. Effectively, Dante Alighieri did exactly this.

In some areas, this is still not enough. In the United States, for example, the IACE has been established: the Italian American Committee on Education. It operates in New York, New Jersey, and Connecticut. Its statute and website illustrate how work and study opportunities are available "thanks to the financial support of the Consulate" and "specifically approved for this purpose."

The need to amplify our cultural offerings can have one of two explanations. Is it possible that from Harlem, the Bronx, and Midtown, as opposed to Midtown, Chinatown, or Greenwich Village, Americans have started to move en masse to Italian schools to the point where our scholastic institutes abroad could not handle such an imposing number of aspiring students? It is possible, though it might seem strange, that there has been no news of this in the international media. Certainly it would have become an important news feature. Or perhaps, the second explanation: this onslaught of "officials" is responsible for ordinary administrative work and therefore if someone truly desired to learn something about Italy or even its language, they would have to turn elsewhere.

The same explanation could be offered for the cultural sector as for the economic sector.

Scattered around the world, at the tax-payer's expense, we have valid teachers, qualified workers, valid professors and managers that could truly transform our language, art, and museums into a billion dollar industry. Unfortunately, they are forced to operate alongside an army of imbeciles (with college degrees) and academic braggarts whose failures have been well documented by decades' worth of salaries and reimbursements that have been completely unproductive.

Considering how many of these people we have scattered around the world promoting Italy and the Italian language, our typographers should all be busy day and night printing grammar manuals and dictionaries.

Instead, the Italian language is losing ground in our own country. Never mind teaching our language to foreigners.

Our children no longer speak our language and prefer to speak a sort of syncopated language that is littered with English and foreign slang. Why waste time learning the subjunctive and conditional clauses? They believe it is easier to fall back upon the infinitive because it is more direct and more efficient: it is more immediately expressive.

They believe that speaking, without literary curlicues, should allow for immediate comprehension.

In addition to the vast number of Italian offices abroad, when the regions were established they concluded that they could not adequately carry out their duties without sufficient representation in Brussels.

Near the European Parliament, 20 delegations set up camp. Twenty offices, sometimes even extremely costly ones with a considerable amount of employees that occupy themselves with following political and administrative activities. Their main task is to amass the funds that are made available to them.

Initially, this job was viewed as a highly competitive one. Each region decided to accumulate as many funds as possible without much concern for its neighbor (despite being fellow countrymen). The result was that we were behind in our efforts in comparison to the Spanish, French, Germans, and even the Portuguese, who all managed to act as teams. So we realized that we had to make amends and form a consortium with the creation of an institute that should have catered to the interest of all 20 regions that alone were incapable of operating on their own.

The offices vying for funds became 21.

The Campania region, up until a few months ago, had its own separate office in New York. There are numerous Neapolitans in the USA and many have become successful. The Festival of San Gennaro in Little Italy is a celebration of faith, nostalgia, and generosity with a great amount of participation from the local Neapolitans. But what purpose does a regional office in the United States serve?

CHAPTER 5

A COUNTRY HANGING OVER THE VOID

We should have found a way to reform our Constitution years ago so that we could have assured that it was more up to date with the evolution of our time. This is how things happen in the rest of the world.

Instead, when we began speaking about the need to initiate a process of change (late) that touched the fundamental governmental institutions of the country, voices in the choir emerged stating that we lived in the best world possible. The defense of our Constitution appeared to be dictated more by our ideology than by any theoretical reasoning pertaining to law. This is politicking, for sure, and not in the least bit concrete.

The first defense, a strenuous and resolute one, came from university professors of constitutional law. In and of themselves, these professors represent a sort of small caste. They don't behave much differently from a tavern owner who when asked if his wine is good, assures his customers that there is no better wine to be found anywhere nearby.

Their publications have begun to fill the bookstores in order to explain the Constitution to children, and to reassure them that it was "created to unite" and asserting that it is "friendly," healthy, and "robust."

The former singer of the Rokes, Shel Shapiro, set the first 11 articles of the Constitution to music. His Italian is certainly not that of a native Italian despite his having lived here for several decades. His intentions were noble. He realized that youngsters today are distracted and inattentive. They do not study in school and do not even know the history of their own country, the judicial traditions, or the administrative principles. Imagine if the teachers would even bother to illustrate the basic elements of the Constitution.... Instead, he thought it should be a text that is loved and should be divulged as much as possible. He believed that music could be the proper vehicle to rouse the most awareness amongst teenagers. If anything it is curious to note that in the video posted on *Repubblica.it* where Shapiro presented his celebratory song regarding the Italian Constitution, he is sitting in front of an American flag.

Shapiro's initiative happened almost at the same time as a program by Roberto Benigni aired on television. He presented the Constitution as "the most beautiful one in the world."

They all sing and praise, like enamored fetishists, the grace of a law that should simply be observed and respected and not loved, adored, or kissed.

Ruffian pedagogy does not help our country and does not allow for growth either.

Should we expect a rap ballad regarding our Court of Auditors? Or perhaps a rock concert regarding the law enforcement system? Maybe a sweet song regarding the Drivers' Manual?

In the 1950s, with a sociological acceleration comparable to a three-speed Vespa, our Constitution could have seemed redundant, slow, rhetorical, and even excessive though still feasible. To travel from Milan to Rome one needed 33 hours. By train. People sang: "I wander about the city alone" and it was a liberating phrase. The perils of war were no more and people no longer feared reprisals. The roads were once again open to use by everyone and the streetlamps were once again lit.

Sacrifices became acceptable and they no longer seemed so unmanageable because the only means of comparison was the war. Speculation was not a substitute for action. Quality of life had not yet substituted the value of life itself.

The man who best represented this rebirth was the survivor and the man that most exemplified this notion was cyclist Fausto Coppi. One made due with American cigarettes that could be purchased individually or in packets. In amusement parks one could shoot with rifles that fired corks and the winners were awarded with a bottle of *Cinzano*.

The walls were decorated with posters from banks that offered the "national loan for the reconstruction effort."

The country seemed divided. On one hand, it was posed for the future but on the other it seemed quite rooted in its past. It was tempted by the modern age, but appeared to be held back by its ancestral history. The more advanced cities seemed to want to break from tradition. The outskirts seemed to be more conservative. It was jealous of the myths it harbored and would not cede even a millimeter precisely because they were contested.

But even with delays, flaws, bigotry, and contradictions the country was happy. People laughed and sang the way they no longer do today. If anything, today the people are unseemly. They no longer sing and passively delegate this task to the latest version of their iPod.

Italy ran a little and walked a little. Towns expanded, cities grew, and the lira won Oscars because the international community considered it to be a dependable currency. Those days are long gone. They were different times.

The country of common folk undertook the road towards development. The country of Sophists remained trapped in the stitching of a shirt ever more similar to the Tunic of Nessus. To the "partisans" it all seemed exquisite. The fabric seemed to be of good quality, the color seemed bright and the style seemed nice and acceptable. But that tunic was not to be worn: it would mean certain death by asphyxiation.

That outdated Constitution is absolutely harmful. All of those passages between the Prime Minister, the Quirinale Palace, Parliament, and the Constitutional Court; all of that going back and forth several times over for each single decision; all of those charlatan-like procedures contribute to miring the issues and only widen the gap between the "legal" country and the "real" country.

Law and institution reform should have happened at least 30 years ago. But the ruling class concurred that everything was going quite well for them and that they should continue in the same fashion. They were too busy warming their seats on *Montecitorio* and in *Palazzo Madama...* why should they change anything?

Giuseppe Tomasi di Lampedusa, with extraordinary foresight, identified the constant to which our character would remain faithful to over the course of the centuries: proposing and encouraging radical changes, with the condition that everything remain exactly the same. An entire ruling class managed to traverse, at a quick pace, the Republics of the modern age and all of the traps that went along with them. They managed to survive, and not too badly at that: why should they desire to adopt new political systems?

In fact, they do all they can to assure us that they do not want to change.

Silvio Berlusconi wanted change, though his intentions did not go beyond his words. His words were mere chatter, but they appeared to be credible chatter. His words appeared to have some concrete value. There was even a Minister of Simplification. His name was Roberto Calderoli and he was a member of the *Lega* party. He had even drawn up a bill that involved significantly reducing the number of deputies and senators. Each chamber would be reduced to 250 members. He also proposed to delineate the duties of the Parliament members and to transform the Senate into a Federal Senate. Perhaps it is a coincidence but during the final stretch to get the bill passed, all the men of the majority party that were to vote on the reform came down with "stomachaches" .The blame was diverted to Berlusconi and his sexual forays as well as his dialectic slipups. Each mistake, real or presumed, became fodder for international debate. *The Economist*'s stories went around the world several times over.

All of this was useless and much time and effort were wasted.

One does not touch the Constitution and all of the legislative and bureaucratic machines wound up accepting and reproducing this model. The result of this is that each administrative act seems burdened by a large sense of accomplishment that continues to grow.

Each passage is burdened by bureaucratic language that often renders it difficult to decipher even for those experts whose job is to execute the task. An interpreter is always needed. This legal jargon is still widely accepted and used and often the main text is supplemented with a "*sub*" or an "*infra*" according to its position in the amendment.

The bureaucratic offices are in the hands of a group of officials who live in a world that they themselves built and that they worry about further consolidating as it is: perfect (probably) in form but (certainly) inapplicable in its substance and anyway thousands of miles away from the truth. They behave like the Mandarins in Imperial China: they write in "legalese" that is classic and faultless. Afterwards, they await the compliments of their professors, who declare with mouths agape that they admire the lucidity of the written doctrine. Without fail, after the Official Gazette has been published, a law that has about a dozen articles (which in and of themselves are too many) produces a tome with approximately one hundred attachments to "interpret" that masterpiece of legal science that undoubtedly needs numerous explications that are geared towards those who will have to apply them. It is not rare that these explanations need further explaining with more specifications.

Gian Luca Rana, the son of Giovanni Rana who is known by the public for his tortellini and the commercials that followed, in a brief interview managed to illustrate Italy's fatigue. This country cannot run and has trouble walking as well. He had wanted to build a factory in Verona, where the company's headquarters is also located. At the same time, he wanted to build a factory in Chicago as well. They predicted that they would begin production at around the same time. In the United States, after ten and a half months, the factory was operative. In Italy, the factory took seven years of paperwork, stamps, and authorizations.

"In the United States," he recounted, "it was sufficient to present our project along with five signatures and in fifteen days we received our authorization. In Italy, each minimal modification requires ten copies of the document along with a signature for each copy, a stamp, and a notification. In Chicago, the police and fire departments came and asked us if we needed any help and they offered us some advice."

What does the fire department in Italy do?

The *Sole 24 ore* newspaper has estimated that Italian bureaucracy costs our small businesses 26 billion euro. This is the value of a holding company or at least the amount that would be sufficient to offer a decent salary to all those that are unemployed who uselessly knock on the doors of businesses seeking jobs that they never seem to find. It is this very additional cost that justifies international companies in their decision to snub Italy. It is also what pushes other Italian companies to move their headquarters abroad.

We had initially believed that these relocations happened towards countries that offered cheaper labor with fewer taxes. In reality, the companies that left often went to Innsbruck where the workers earn similar wages as in Italy but there are fewer administrative difficulties that transform these businesses into a slippery slope.

What is the benefit of saving a half-hour of time taking the road between Civitavecchia and Grosseto if then one must wait 10 years for the resolution of a civil lawsuit, 2 years to know whether a judge will decide to give a worker a job back, and over 1 year to be paid by the public administration?

In order to select 147 technical managers in the scholastic systems, five years were required to publish the list of the candidates that had passed the written exam and that therefore had the right to continue onto the next phase, which was the oral exam. Who knows how many of those candidates in the meantime died or retired?

With all of these obstacles, knots, and snarls, this country remains dangling over the void.

Part II

150 Years of Unified Taxes

CHAPTER 1

THE DEAF, LAME, STUTTERERS, AND THE HUNCHBACK

The only constant over the course of the 150 years of Italy's Unification concerns the increase in the number of members of Parliament and in their privileges. Each time an increase occurred, an exponential growth in the amount of taxes owed also occurred in order to cover the expense of a public debt in constant expansion. Nothing, and I mean absolutely nothing, has been done to reduce these expenses in order to re-establish the balance to an acceptable level. They have not even tried.

In this respect, the taxes levied by the Monti administration are coherent with the political context dating back to the Risorgimento. It is perfectly coherent.

The taxes that the Italians are currently dealing with in 2012 and 2013 are nothing more than the most recent installment, though perhaps not the last, of a public debt that began growing with Camillo Benso the Count of Cavour and his administrations.

Our troubles have their roots in our history.

The first Parliament of the new kingdom denounced, from the very beginning, all of the faults that over time managed only to become more severe. All that angers us today has only gotten worse starting from 1861. One of the first complaints was the vast number of representatives that worked in the public sector.

Ferdinando Petruccelli della Gattina, who possessed both a poisonous tongue and pen, realized this almost immediately. In an article he wrote for the *La Presse* newspaper in Paris he stated: "The Italian government is composed of 433 representatives. Aside from 7 resignations and 5 deaths which do not figure into the equation there are 2 princes, 3 dukes, 29 counts, 23 marquis, 26 barons, 50 commanders, and

117 knights of which 3 are also members of the Legion of Honor. Then there are also: 135 lawyers, 25 doctors, 21 engineers, and 10 priests including Apollo Sanguineti, one of the Prime Minister's primary nuisances, and Ippolito Amicarelli and Flaminio Valente who are more quiet priests. Additionally, we also have 4 admirals, 23 generals, 13 magistrates, 52 professors or former professors (or at least those who claim as much)." This is an enormous amount of "representatives". Are they all really necessary?

"There is a Bey from the Ottoman Empire, the Honorable Paternostro, 2 former dictators, 2 former dictatorship supporters, 19 former ministers, 6 or 7 millionaires, 25 members of the nobility with no titles, 4 sole writers and Verdi, Maestro Verdi that is."[1]

The only one missing was Carlo Cattaneo who preferred to create his own Parliament "by himself, in his own home." He was in contrast with the Savoy Italy that was inspired by centralized, authoritarian models. He was elected 3 times and 3 times he refused to swear his loyalty to the Savoys.[2] He actually made a few scathing critical remarks against what he considered to be the "government of servants" promoted by Turin. "It is as though we have fought not to have more freedom but rather to descend even further into the regime of servitude."

Petruccelli della Gattina considered himself to be part of the opposition and did not tolerate the useless rituals of Parliamentary rhetoric. The representatives of his people inflated themselves with their arrogance and altruism in order to democratically find tyrannical solutions. "We have news concerning 6 stutterers, 5 deaf people, 3 lame persons, a hunchback, many people with eyeglasses, many bald people, but no mutes!" Everyone spoke and they made sure not to skimp on words.

By analyzing the dynamics of the Parliament of the time, it is not difficult to find many similarities to the Parliament today, especially regarding political attitudes. Sometimes even identical proposals are made,

---

[1] F. Petruccelli Della Gattina, *I moribondi del Palazzo Carignano* (Milan, 1962).
[2] R. Bracalini, *Carlo Cattaneo, un federalista per gli italiani* (Milan, 1995).

though many of these were mistakes then and continue to be so now as well.

The representatives elected during the former Kingdom of the Two Sicilies were to be found more or less at the political center of the political scheme of the Parliament. Petruccelli della Gattina believed that the Center was the "life raft of the Medusa": that place where "all those who have been shipwrecked, the survivors, are holding onto for their lives." The center had taken on the form of a sort of "hospice for those invalids who no longer had strength, but not for this reason did they abandon all hope."[3]

The Left, although greatly reduced, seemed to be an archipelago of suffering souls and was mostly comprised of "those supporters of Mazzini and Garibaldi, the autonomists and the federalists, those who lived on the other side of the mountains, the free, the employed, and the independent." There were those loners who also had their own weight in Parliament: "the mysterious, the undecided, the sullen and the lost, the skeptics, the doctrinaires, the pretenders, the explorers of enemy territories, as well as those one might consider migrant birds."

"Migrant birds:" this is how Petruccelli della Gattina defined with his imaginative language "several of those from the extreme Left that, though resolved to pass to the Right, managed to—how can one say?— stop in the middle, on the benches of the Left." Are there any names? "Chiaves and Gallenca: the second of which has already made progress and now sits at the center."[4]

With his writing, which was both irreverent and biting, Petruccelli della Gattina ruined many old friendships and was forced to end many established relationships. He found himself facing three duel challenges, but yet he managed to find a definition of the Parliament that is quite timeless: though the names of the people may change, the situations and

---

[3] F. Petruccelli Della Gattina, *I moribondi del Palazzo Carignano* (Milan, 1962).
[4] Ibid.

even the details are identical regardless of monarchies or republics, beyond the Unification of Italy on the threshold of the third millennium.

Interestingly enough, the writings of Petruccelli della Gattina were published in a book entitled *I moribondi di palazzo Carignano* (*The Dying Men of Palazzo Carignano*). Today, they would be the dying men of which building?

The Parliament of 1861 should have had the enthusiasm to renew Italian society. Instead, it had an incredibly decrepit attitude before it even began to work for the country. The newly formed State seemed destined to advance to the future more by inertia than by any actual conviction.

Of the 433 members of elected Parliamentarians, only 27 could actually be placed in areas that opposed their presence and even amongst those, loopholes were found so that they could not carry out their duties. For example, the Sicilian Gregorio Ugdulena, a somewhat bizarre person that managed to pull off being a Liberal Pro-Garibaldi priest was loved by the public. For him, or more appropriately "just" for him, an old law was dusted off that stated that in Piedmont, members of the clergy were not allowed to hold public office. Consequently, he could not perform his assigned tasks and his mandate was left to expire. This is in spite of the fact that there were at least another dozen or so priests that, since they were in favor of the government in power, managed to hold on to their positions. Laws created explicitly for and against specific people have been around for quite some time.

Vito Di Nardo, in writing his work *Oh, mia patria* concluded that Cavour had been declared the sole victor by having knocked out all of his adversaries:[5] Leftists, clergymen, and Pro-Monarchists. This result had lasting effects. The Left required 16 years before it managed to even rear its head. The Catholics, once they had finished their protest by abstention, needed to wait for Don Luigi Sturzo before they managed to enter the

---

[5] V. Di Nardo, *Oh, mia Patria. Un inviato speciale nel primo anno dell'unità d'Italia* (Milan, 1990).

political arena once again. Those who had supported the monarchies definitively disappeared from politics and did not even have the right to voice their opinions despite not having any elected members of Parliament.[6]

The representatives of that first legislature of the Kingdom of Italy met for the inaugural session of Parliament on March 14, 1861. Upon a close examination, they seemed inadequate from the very beginning.

They began by debating whether elected military officials could present themselves in Parliament in uniform.[7] This problem is completely irrelevant compared to more pressing matters at hand but nevertheless was taken quite seriously. A long, bitter debate ensued. A uniform could not be worn "without the instruments that justified its presence" in other words, a sword. But the government needed to be a place where one could freely debate one's opinion and therefore should not host armed men. They finally concluded that those elected military officials should wear common clothes, just the same as the other representatives.

Then they proceeded to debate compensation for elected officials. Minghetti decided, and he communicated the outcome to the newspapers, that there would be no compensation for elected officials, not even in the form of reimbursement for expenses incurred. "The Statute excludes this as a notion, " he curtly stated, "otherwise the Parliament would embark upon a dangerous path." Furthermore, any representatives and senators that "profited" from their elected offices were invited either to resign their position or give up the activity that was garnering them a profit, and therefore a conflict of interest. Everyone found themselves in agreement and emphasized how important and just such a decision was. All those elected officials nodded their heads quite emphatically, with very serious expressions on their faces to demonstrate that such an important issue had found an adequate solution.

---

[6] *Translator's note*: this is often a courtesy right granted to those no longer having elected members.

[7] *Gazzetta del Popolo*, February 28, March 4 and 7, 1861.

In reality, Francesco Crispi continued to offer his legal advice to those bankers of the Weill-Schott company of Milan and Florence even when they attempted to buy into the Italian State's tobacco monopoly. And to continue in the vein of "conflicts of interest,[8]" Cimone Weill-Schott signed any comments he made regarding the economy (or at least those that were in his own or his company's best interest) in Crispi's newspaper *La riforma*.

Bixio, a general and a representative, did not leave his position on the administration board of the Institute of Real Estate Credit and did not feel embarrassed when it came time to collect the dividends, even if the Institute had obtained contracts for State funded projects.

Gustavo Cavour, brother of the Prime Minister, was one of the majority shareholders of the *Cassa di Sconto* (a bank from Turin) and that with English funds, managed to obtain the contract to build the canal that would bring water to the lower part of the area surrounding Novara and in the Lomellina area to irrigate the rice fields. It is not by chance that this channel appears on maps as the "Cavour Channel." The Cavour family was considered extremely "capable of making profit."[9] The very honest Bettino Ricasoli charged 80,000 piasters in order to grant his permission to allow the railroad to pass through a wooded area on his property.[10]

This is all idle chatter and gossip. This is all pure speculation. In 150 years, has anything actually changed?

[8] *Gazzetta del Popolo*, March 5 and 6, 1861.
[9] N. Dobroljulov, *Conti, preti, briganti* (Milan, 1966).
[10] R. Bracalini, *L'Italia prima dell'unità (1815-1860)* (Milan, 2001).

CHAPTER 2

THE USELESS AND COSTLY SENATORS OF THE KING

Today, there are 945 members of Parliament: 630 representatives and 315 senators. We must also add those senators "for life": in other words former Presidents and a few eminent public figures that the Quirinale retains appropriate to "reward" with a senatorial position.

Putting aside an individual's worth and personal prestige, this phenomenon renders the Italian government unique in the planet's political scheme. In the United States, former presidents have returned to cultivating their family's peanut plantations, taking care of the family ranch, selling crude oil, or even proposing themselves as public speakers for conferences for which they are handsomely paid, but not with the money of American tax-payers. Why is it necessary to offer our former Presidents a position in the Senate when they are often gentlemen in their eighties? They have already enjoyed generous salaries, receive large pensions as well as guaranteed life annuities. Is it really necessary to guarantee them an additional salary?

Besides keeping their seats warm in Palazzo Madama, what concrete contribution have former Presidents (such as Cossiga, Scalfaro, and Ciampi) made? In the legislative sphere, what proposals, interventions, or contributions have been made, over the course of decades, by the likes of Giovanni Agnelli, Carlo Bo, Pininfarina, and Rita Levi Montalcini? The Senate's meetings are so desperately desolate because the authorities in their fields (to the point of warranting a Nobel Prize) are completely useless on the political playing field. In some instances, they have merely served to ensure the party majority of Romano Prodi's administration.

The figure of a senator for life is a vestige of the era of monarchies when the Senate members were directly appointed by the sovereign. In

Italy today, we can no longer afford such regal privileges. We should forget replacing those senators for life who have already died: we should seriously be entertaining the notion that the species should be abolished.

There are too many elected members of Parliament as well. The United States manage to function with 435 representatives and 99 senators that are presided over by the Vice President, which brings the total to 100. Proportionately, we should be able to make do with 104.4 representatives and 23.76 senators. Great Britain has one legislative chamber with 650 members. France elects 577 representatives and 346 senators. China, with its 1 billion and a half of inhabitants, has a Parliament composed of 3,000 members that meet only once a year, at the beginning of March, to ratify the decisions that have already been adopted by the Communist party.

The nearly 1000 Parliament members in Italy, since 1945, have managed to consolidate themselves as a sort of "caste"[11] whose defining characteristic is irremovability.

With rare exceptions, either God in Heaven decides to remove them from their position or no one resigns from the position that they have obtained. The Italian political class is amongst the ones with the longest life span and it is the most outdated. It is also the class that is the most attached to its seat to the point of defending its position tooth and nail against any adversary who might call their authority into question.[12]

Only when they are no longer able to stay in Rome do these "dethroned" politicians attempt to find some other "seat" to fall back on. In the end, there is always an extra seat available somewhere: in the Region, as mayor of their town, in some completely pointless institution that has a position with a decent salary. The CNEL (The National Council for

---

[11] G.A. Stella and S. Rizzo, *La casta: così i politici italiani sono diventati intoccabili* (Milan, 2007).

[12] F. De Feo, "L'unico vero posto fisso? Quello del parlamentare. Il Paese è ostaggio di una gerontocrazia inchiodata alta poltrona e in carica da decenni. Solo uno su tre è alla prima legislatura. I casi La Malfa e Pisanu, a Palazzo da 40 anni" in *Il Giornale*, June 15, 2012.

Economy and Labor) is composed of 121 members that each have a large salary and all expenses paid: it costs a fortune to operate and offers consultations that no one ever bothers to read. The task of managing the Port of Cagliari was given to Piergiorgio Massidda, a senator of the PDL party and an excellent plastic surgeon. The management of another 12 important ports were assigned to those who were forced away from the capital: the Port of Savona was assigned to an ex representative of the Forza Italia party, Piombino was assigned to a former mayor from the DS party, Catania was assigned to a councilor from the AN party, and Salerno was assigned to the former undersecretary of the PD party.[13]

The list of "strange" government-funded institutions is quite long and accounts for a great amount of wasteful expenses. The Agronomic Institute for Overseas Ventures is an organ of the Ministry of Foreign Affairs. It has its headquarters in Florence and employs one general director and a staff of 47 people. It designs masters programs for Irrigation Systems in Pakistan or guarantees the irrigation of palm trees in Libyan oases.[14] The EIUT, on the other hand, is the Umbrian-Tuscan Irrigation Institute. It was actually closed, but only for two months.[15] The National Association for the Testing of Firearms of Gardone-Val Trompia seemed as though it were to be the next government affiliated entity to be shut down, but it merely changed its address. Now it is a guest of the Chamber of Commerce. The Ministry of Economic Development nominates 12 members to its board of administration to carry out its programs. A volume that celebrates its 100 years of activity was recently published.[16]

There are around 34,000 government funded entities that are considered "useless" but, despite a declaration that explicitly states their complete and utter inefficiency, there is no way to shut them down. The Minister of "Simplification" Roberto Calderoli took his assigned task

---

[13] F. Bechis, "La casta si ricicla in dodici porti sicuri" in *Libero*, September 29, 2011.
[14] M. Giordano, *Spudorati. La grande beffa dei costi della politica: false promesse e verità nascoste* (Milan, 2012).
[15] Ibid.
[16] Ibid.

seriously and tried to make some cuts but he was forced to throw in the towel. After months of trying he was able to shut down 24 of these entities, which is equivalent to around .06%: practically nothing. The others exerted a serious effort to continue to exist: the National Institute for the Children of Aviators, the Foundation for Vesuvian Villas, the Vittorio Emanuele III National Institute for Charity, the ARSEA of Catania (Institute to Facilitate the Distribution of Subsidies to Farmers), and the National Center for Typology which moved from Bologna to Catanzaro.

Each one of these entities has a board of directors, employees, a budget and expenses.

But certainly the Parliament in Rome is the primary objective, and once there, the members of Parliament establish their roots.

In the entire world, the governments change and the faces of those who govern change. Here, the faces remain unchanged. They alternate between being members of the majority party and the opposition.

The men of the Center-Right, perhaps victims of their own individualism, over the course of time managed to develop a sort of bland admiration for Margaret Thatcher and Ronald Reagan. The Center-Left, on the other hand, managed to fall in love with every leader that had any vaguely Communist ideologies: they debuted with their love for Kennedy, and then veered towards Clinton. They cheered for Lula, fancied Zapatero, were inspired by Blair, found an example in Gorbachev and finally elected Obama as their mentor. It was just about to include the French President Hollande to its team of role models when his popularity took a nose dive. This halted their enthusiasm.

Each of these international leaders had their rise and fall in power and exhausted their physical life cycle, once again returning to their private lives. Those here in Italy continue to praise the new members who rise to power, while remaining comfortably in their seats. They are a Jurassic generation that has seen the geological era of politics and, both obstinately and tirelessly, continues to repeatedly propose themselves and their recipes as the solution to the government's problems.

The projects that they promote become lost amidst the government's paperwork and the titles of the books they publish with the assistance of some collaborator. They refer to the "strong and free,"[17] imagine a "civil Italy"[18], they believe that they are proposing "a good reason,"[19] they open a dialogue with "the Northeast,"[20] or they know the solutions of our "neighbors in the Orient."[21] They know where the "emergency exits"[22] are located. They propose to rebuild their political party[23] and offer politics "in the age of globalization."[24] On paper they have solutions for everything. I'd be damned if, of the many ideas they have put forward in all the time that they have been in power, they managed to put even one of those ideas into effect.

They were incapable of reducing their salary and yet, after having slaughtered that of every other mortal, you would think that they would have learned how to efficiently do this.

The appanage of the Parliament was not even trimmed after the intervention of a highly specialized committee. It took 4 months, 5 fully attended meetings, and a 37-page report, but in the end, nothing was to be done. Masterminds of statistics and economy were employed, headed by Enrico Giovannini, the President of ISTAT (the National Institute for Statistics). He was followed by the professor/lawyer Alfonso Celotto (professor of constitutional law at the University Roma Tre), Professor Ugo Trivellato (Professor Emeritus of Statistical Economy at the University of Padua), Professor Giovanni Valotti (Professor of Business Economy and Public Administration at the Bocconi University), and the professor/lawyer Alberto Zito (Professor of Administrative Law at the

---

[17] M. Sacconi, *Ai liberi e forti* (Milan, 2011).

[18] G. Fini, *Un'Italia civile (intervista di Marcello Staglieno)* (Milan, 1999).

[19] P. Bersani, *Per una buona ragione* (Bari, 2011).

[20] G. De Michelis and M. Sacconi, *Dialogo a Nordest. Sul futuro dell'Italia fra Europa e Mediterraneo* (Venice, 2010).

[21] O. Diliberto, *Vicino Oriente* (Reggio Emilia, 2005).

[22] G. Tremonti, *Uscita di sicurezza* (Milan, 2012).

[23] O. Diliberto, *Ricostruire il partito. Appunti per una discussione* (Macerata, 2011).

[24] M. D'Alema, *La politica ai tempi della globalizzazione* (Lecce, 2003).

University of Teramo). None of these gentlemen were able to bring the salary level of the Italian Parliament to that of their European colleagues "with the accuracy required by the Law."[25]

Therefore, Italy's representatives and senators continue to make 16,000 Euro each month. The French stop at 13,000 Euro, the Germans at 12,000 Euro, the Dutch at 10,000, the Belgians at 9,000 Euro, the Austrians at 8,000 Euro, and the Spanish at 4,000 Euro. This ranges from an average of 20% to 400% more than our European colleagues. It is a record, and in this we are absolutely in first place without any direct competition.

There are those who believe that a salary of that level is insufficient. Gerardo Bianco, who was a representative up until the beginning of the third millennium and who is now the President of the Association of Former Members of Parliament, declared that their monthly salaries were barely sufficient to cover expenses.[26] Lorenzo Cesa, secretary of the UDC party founded by Pierferdinando Casini, actually proposed to raise the salary. It happened that his colleague, Cosimo Mele, wound up in a hotel room with two girls, one of which suffered a drug overdose and required hospitalization. Cesa invented the notion of increasing the amount allotted for travel expenses by including an "anti-temptation"[27] clause so that Parliament members could travel to Rome with their families so as to avoid the temptation of Rome's nighttime entertainment. The idea immediately roused controversy. The proposal's most outward detractor was then President of the Chamber of Deputies, Fausto Bertinotti. He declared the initiative to be "immoral" but did not once propose to lower

---

[25] M. Giordano, "Onorevoli stipendi intoccabili: si arrendono anche i cervelloni. Costi della politica: la commissione Giovannini rinuncia. Dovevano studiare il taglio delle retribuzioni ai deputati italiani per ridurli ai livelli dell'Europa. Mesi di "intenso lavoro" poi il responso: impossibile. Ma non si poteva fare come con le pensioni?" in *Il Giornale*, April 5, 2012.

[26] M. Giordano, Spudorati. *La grande beffa dei costi della politica: false promesse e verità nascoste* (Milan, 2012).

[27] G .A. Stella, "Ultima frontiera dei privilegi: un'indennità contro le tentazioni. La proposta di Cesa. Onorevoli spesso lontani da casa? Le sedute in media 3 alla settimana" in *Corriere della Sera*, July 31, 2007.

the salaries of the Parliament members to the level of the average citizen.[28] Montecitorio and Palazzo Madama remain a world unto themselves.

To be honest, aside from the paycheck that each member singularly receives each month, the expenses that the political "caste" incurs are completely outrageous.

The Prime Minister's Office has 4,600 employees. The Cabinet Office, the English equivalent, manages with 1,337. Why are there three times as many people employed in Rome? Palazzo Chigi spends 5.6 million euro for receptions and conventions, 11 million "the facilitation of decisional processes and efficiency", 3.5 million for the "organizational wellbeing of its employees" (in other words a sort of club for its employees), and 938,000 for a structure that assigns the vehicles to be used for the Parliament's official car service.[29] The 340,000 euro allotted to spot and eliminate wasteful spending are completely wasted.

Between 2006 and 2011, the expenses increased by 46%. In 2012, those expenses increased by another 2.5%.

The Chamber of Deputies saw its expenses increase by 41% between 2011 and 2012. In 2012, they cut down on cleaning expenses: they had previously had a budget of 7,730,000 euro and they cut it down to 7,610,000. So they spent 120,000 euro less on toilet paper.[30]

The Senate's expenses grew by 65% and in 2012 they managed to reduce this amount by 0.34%. At Palazzo Madama, 3 million euro are spent for their restaurant, 1.2 million for the telephone bill, 500,000 euro for office supplies, 160,000 for linens, and 20,000 euro for utensils and dishes.[31]

---

[28] G.A. Stella, "Immorale! Bertinotti boccia la proposta di Cesa di concedere più emolumenti ai deputati per favorire la riunione delle famiglie" in *Corriere della Sera*, August 1, 2007.
[29] E. Fittipaldi, "Gli sprechi di Palazzo Silvio" in *L'Espresso*, August 25, 2011.
[30] G. De Marchis, "Le spese della Camera sfondano il miliardo" in *la Repubblica*, August 17, 2011.
[31] P. Di Nicola, "Un Parlamento tutto d'oro" in *L'Espresso*, December 21, 2011.

For the government's expenses, each Italian spends approximately 27.35 Euro versus the 14.42 spent by the French, 13.84 by the Germans, 11.45 by the Americans, and 9.90 by the English. The other Europeans spend even less and Spain spends 4.80 euro, the most modest amount.

The salaries, extra benefits, bonuses, and special titles all weigh heavily on the budget. The Chamber and Senate have a president and 8 vice-presidents. Each perceives a monthly bonus of 5,149 euro and receives special lodging along with extra personnel. The same privilege is extended for the 6 commissioners and their 24 secretaries. Presidents of committees only receive access to car service, a secretary, and a 3,316 euro bonus.

These financial advantages reverberate, in proportion, to the rest of the political palaces ranging from the presidencies to the doormen. In these cases, a contract is offered that has no rivals in the rest of the world. In the Chamber of Deputies, a low-level technician (rather than a barber or a chauffeur) receives a monthly salary that ranges from 2,300 euro to 9,461. In the Senate, a simple clerk earns 8,000 euro, and a filing clerk earns 12,000 euro, while a secretary earns 15,000 euro. A parliamentary stenographer could find himself with a salary of 259,000 euro a year, as much as the President of the United States.

These salaries are astronomical because the mechanisms of regulation that are implemented for other workers are not applied to those employed by government institutions. For those employed by the State, the only measures applied include the triennial adaptation to inflation and the automatic biennial promotion. These adaptations were in effect since before 1984 before they were blocked by then Prime Minister Bettino Craxi. The Communist party attempted to hold a referendum to recuperate them but those funds definitively left the pockets of workers. Well, all those workers except those employed by the Chamber of Deputies and the Senate. This was the era of Trapattoni coaching Juventus and whose star player was Michel Platini. The Oscars that year were dominated by Robert Duvall, Shirley MacLaine, and *Terms of Endearment*. Silvio Berlusconi had not yet decided to enter politics. This was another time period. The result is that the paychecks of those lucky few grew quickly, and over the course of forty years they multiplied 4.2 times over. This condition seems entirely indefensible. Yet the 14 unions that defend the rights of those employed by the State seem quite decided upon defending their rights to the bitter end.

The numbers, therefore, are large and disproportionate. The Chamber of Deputies has 1,642 employees and the Senate has 940 plus an unspecified amount of short-term contract employees. This means that for the Chamber of Deputies, the services offered by the personnel come to 288,940,000 euro while the Senate "gets by" with spending 139,470,000 euro.

To host such an army of members of Parliament and State employees, Montecitorio and Palazzo Madama are not sufficient. The use of another 42 buildings scattered between the Colosseum and the Vatican is necessary. This amounts to a space of 250,000 square meters, four times the size of the Louvre.

Here we offer a comparison: at the Bundestag in Berlin, 600 representatives occupy 3 buildings that amount to 11,000 square meters (one twentieth of the Italian Parliament's space!). In Paris, the Assemblée Nationale makes due with two buildings: one for legislative work and the other for services. In London, Westminster is sufficient.

Our Parliament occupies 35 buildings: 21 for our representatives and 14 for our senators. Ten buildings are the property of Palazzo Chigi. The last buildings to be added are those located on Via dei Laterani, Via della Vite, Via dell'Umiltà, and Via della Ferrarella. Comically, the Ministry for Simplification was to have its headquarters located in Piazza San Lorenzo in Lucina.

It seems as though it is impossible for us to save any room. It is necessary to assign an office and an apartment of 200 square meters for each former president from each of the two branches of the Parliament. This means that from the Chamber of Deputies Irene Pivetti, Luciano Violante, Fausto Bertinotti, and Pierferdinando Casini have a small neighborhood at their disposal. The same goes for the Senators Carlo Scognamiglio, Nicola Mancino, Marcello Pera, and Franco Marini. The private offices of Gianfranco Fini and Renato Schifani have already been prepared. The representative Franco Barbato of the Italia dei Valori party, with a small video camera hidden in his jacket's lapel, filmed these little apartments that were a sort of top secret because they are considered to be "personal residences" and therefore completely inaccessible. Each apartment has approximately 7 or 8 rooms with 3 or 4 secretaries, antique furniture, ancient statues, visible historic wooden beams, exotic flowers and plant, and terraces that stretched over the rooftops of Rome.[32]

The rental costs of these buildings incur an expense of 150 million euro per year. The case of the former hotel Bologna caused a small scandal because the Senate had refused to purchase the structure for 23 million euro and preferred to rent it in 2013 for an amount of 32 million euro: in other words 9 million euro more than it would have cost to purchase the property.[33]

Actually, the cost of rentals is the least of the expenses. One must take into consideration the sum of the other expenses. Apartments used as offices that are at the disposal of members of Parliament and their employees must be heated in the winter and cooled in the summer. They must have lighting and working telephones. They must also be insured and protected because the lives of those representing the public are precious. In order to repair the buttons of their elevators 930,000 euro are spent per year. On the ground level of each building there must be a metal detector that someone must operate and that therefore must receive a salary. There must be police officers watching the entrances and exits and they must operate in eight-hour shifts throughout the course of the day. Three shifts of three men must be employed at each given time. There must also be policemen in the streets....

---

[32] P. Bracalini, "Grand Hotel Montecitorio: Barbato incastra i presidenti. Il deputato-pirata dell'Idv è entrato alla Camera con una telecamera nascosta per svelare le stanze riservate degli ex: per ognuno decine di lussuosi uffici, con statue e mobili d'epoca" in *Il Giornale*, April 3, 2012.

[33] M. Favale, "Trentasei palazzi per il Potere" in *la Repubblica*, August 17, 2011.

On each floor, there are 4 uniformed clerks, each with a tricolor stripe on their left shoulder. They are at the constant disposal of the representative (most of the time just to bring the representative and their guests coffee). They receive a salary that starts at 4,000 euro a month.

The State's expenses have continued to grow enormously. They should have grown in proportion to essential needs and settle on reasonable amounts. Instead, each year, they continue to grow and they force more taxes upon the citizens in order to cover their increases.

This is not a problem of the Italy of recent times or of the Italian Republic. No. This has been the way things have gone since the idea of a Unified Italy was born.

CHAPTER 3

THE TRICOLOR DEBT THAT DATES BACK
TO THE RISORGIMENTO

The "hole" in the State's budget has been around for a long time and the Risorgimento cannot help but take responsibility for its role.

In the 34 years between the fall of Napoleon and the First War of Independence, Piedmont could have demonstrated that it possessed a solid administration. In the 12 years following 1848, in the period of "preparation" the deficit climbed to over one billion lira: 1,024,960,595 Piedmontese Lira (at the time).

The first blow to the State's budget was delivered by the defeat in the First War of Independence.

The war, as is the case with all wars, came along with some frightening costs. Let it be understood: the "human" price we paid with those who were maimed, injured, the families that no longer had financial support, the destroyed fields, the famine that often follows battles... these are all things that no one ever calculates. The hypocrisy of war ensures that the reality of the situation is sugar coated with words that seem studied specifically to hide pain and truth. The dead become the "fallen" with a reassuring image that directly eliminates the drama and suffering associated with death. The "fallen"... that isn't too bad... they can still get up...

Therefore, as far as costs are concerned, I intend those costs that were effectively sustained, that are traceable and from which one can draw a final mathematical sum. For tiny Piedmont, badly defeated in Custoza and Novara, aside from the expenses incurred for their own military campaign, the expenses also included reimbursing Austria for damages. Initially, Vienna requested 250 million in damages, which was an exorbitant amount for Turin's coffers. It settled, however for 75.[34] In order to respect the request, it was necessary to call for the assistance of international banks that were capable of sustaining such a large sum. We were granted 315 million in a loan.

This negotiation crossed paths with the fusion of the Bank of Turin and the Bank of Genoa in a context of conflicts of interest that were all quite murky.[35] The ministers in charge of conducting the negotiations, along with Count Camillo di Cavour (despite no longer being a member of the government, he was involved in the negotiations thanks to the friendships he maintained), were all accused of having usurped legislative power with the only aim of establishing a banking-based form of politics that would benefit only a few financial groups.

The complaints were published in the *La Concordia* newspaper, according to which Cavour had made a profit of "about 150,000 lira" along with the others involved: the Nigra brothers, Count Salmour, and the bankers Defernex and Bolmida.[36] How embarrassing.

Even the periodical *L'Armonia* condemned the way public finance was being conducted at the time. "The minister," it reported, "requests loans and plans taxes. The Parliament discusses, votes, and approves. The citizens merely pay." The newspaper did not spare any ferocious criticism: "We will examine our finances under absolutism and compare them with our finances now that we are free." In reality, this type of comparison was impossible to make. "The rule under absolutist governments consisted in spending less than what was collected. They did not have many tenured professors and economists at their disposal, but in compensation, their banks were full of money." In 1847, the assets were around 41 million that managed to transform into a small "hole" in the balance and then subsequently turned into a chasm. "In six years, from 1848 to 1854, loans were requested that amounted to 503,252,161 lira

---

[34] C. Spellanzon and E. Di Nolfo, *Storia del Risorgimento e dell'unità d'Italia* (Milan, 1933-1965).
[35] A. Viarengo, *Cavour* (Rome, 2010).
[36] Ibid.

with an annual interest that amounted to 28,901,443 lira." This type of finance was clearly taken in a lighthearted manner. "We were in debt for 503 million lira but the State had only managed to collect 418 million. Therefore 85 million lira merely evaporated. Whoever touched those fabulous millions (and someone must have touched them because they were nowhere to be found) is right to advocate this system of loans."[37]

The "evaporation" to which the newspaper was referring did not necessarily refer to a theft, or at least not only a theft. Money evaporated because bankers considered lending money to Turin a risk and therefore waged hefty interest fees that required advanced payment.

There was very little faith in Italy: one needed to attract requests for loans with high interest rates. For every 100 lira by contract, the public coffers received 82-83 but in the balance the entire sum should have been taken into account.

In Italy, no one was inclined to begin new business ventures when good money could be earned by buying treasury bonds. Those who acquired their wealth between 1860 and 1870 did not produce goods and did not increase production of anything.

In compensation, in comparison to the vast majority of citizens, those in power were not shy in dipping their hands into the citizens' pockets.

In the meantime, Cavour had become the Minister of Finance and he was not afraid of the word "taxes", especially if others paid them. He believed that a progressive tax was unacceptable. How could he allow the State to reach its hands into his own pockets, guided by him no less? But he did not hesitate to introduce new taxes and for some he exhumed those introduced by Napoleon and abolished during the Restoration.[38] He thought it best to tax goods aside from property: he chose to tax revenues from industry and professional activities (today these are determined by sector studies).

---

[37] *L'Armonia*, November 20, 1855.
[38] I. De Feo, *Cavour, l'uomo e l'opera* (Milan, 1969).

The amount collected was insufficient and it became necessary to knock on the doors of high finance once again.

With the help of Alexis Lombard from the Odier and Lombard Bank of Geneva and the advice of Emilio and Ippolito de la Rue, Cavour designed a project for convertible mortgage loan for 75 million lira that would be guaranteed by the Sub-Alpine Railways, which were State property. The negotiations with Carl Joachim Hambro, a banker from London, were lengthy but in the end, the paperwork was signed. The conditions, however, were not entirely satisfying. Initially, they had proposed an interest tax of 90%, and while they believed they would settle upon a rate of 86-87%, they had to settle for 85%.[39]

So how would they go about collecting more money? The Parliament decided to make the Church contribute. With the Siccardi Law, many convents were confiscated from the Church, and the State managed to come into possession of an inestimable amount of property. That confiscated treasure should have been administrated by a fund whose manager was to be determined by a law signed by Urbano Rattazzi. Who should be entrusted with the administration of that treasure? Rattazzi's brother.[40]

Luigi Fransoni, the Archbishop of Turin, gave the order to organize a protest and was promptly arrested. The very pious Count Santa Rosa was denied his Last Rites because he had voted favorably upon the laws that confiscated the Church's property and he did not repent. The Archbishop, who was held responsible, was expelled from the town and his wealth was confiscated. The Pope refused to nominate his successor. Twelve years later, the bishop died in exile.

It goes without saying that the confiscated properties were auctioned off and wound up benefitting a few wealthy members of society. What reached Piedmont's coffers? Merely crumbs were collected that were barely sufficient to fund the local administration.

---

[39] C.M. Franzero, *Il conte di Cavour e i suoi banchieri inglesi* (Turin, 1968).
[40] A. Viarengo, *Cavour* (Rome, 2010).

It became necessary to request another international loan. This time, Baron Rothschild underwrote commitments for 66 million lira. In order to recuperate some change they invented other taxes, including those on alcoholic beverages but they were only able to make amends for a few expenses.

Another mountain of millions of lira was sacrificed to Europe that, in the middle of the nineteenth century, represented a myth that seemed impossible to ignore. If the world called, how could one not answer? Piedmont did not realize that it was too small to be considered "big" and elbowed its way up in order to keep up with the other world powers. Imagine, Turin, nestled between the Alps, that had been governed by an uncouth dynasty, that looked as though its borders had been defined by an axe, that believed it could stand next to the British Empire, or the "Czar of all Russia", or Napoleon as equals. Had they remained in their place perhaps they would have maintained a dignified position. By attempting to bite off more than they could chew, they wound up compromising the State's equilibrium. The Republic is currently repeating the Monarchy's mistakes. It believes that because we have been invited to attend the G8 that we are actually the 8th world power and continues to behave as though we were.

In the middle of the nineteenth century, an international war broke out in which Turin had no interests to defend and no advantages to obtain. Nevertheless, it chose to participate.

It happened that a war broke out over the control of a few dozen square kilometers in Crimea, on the shores of the Black Sea. It was viewed as a "planetary" war because it involved all the most important world powers at the time: on one side was the Western Bloc with France, England, and Austria. The Eastern Bloc comprised Russia and several other Balkan countries. The conflict presented itself as one of the many that had previously broken out in that area. The Catholics and the Orthodox Christians were fighting over several sacred sites in the area. Other times, those situations had been placated with agreements that, though they may not have rendered everyone happy, at least offered enough solace as to prompt both sides to lay down their weapons.

In 1854, the tension grew until it became a conflict that set the world's diplomacy into a state of disarray. Historians have long reflected upon the issue and have concluded that there were no evident causes for the conflict and even fewer reasons that would explain why it diffused so extensively in so brief a time.[41]

What about Piedmont? Cavour made the decision to participate in the war. "Made the decision:"[42] quite literally. He offered the army's services to the Western allies without even consulting the Ministries and with the declared opposition of the majority of the Ministers. His policies, and his foreign policies even more so, were elaborated without taking into consideration his colleagues: not even those Ministries who should have been directly involved.

In that particular circumstance, the opinions were in opposition because the advantages seemed excessively remote, difficult to calculate, and impossible to explain.

In April 1855, General Alfonso La Marmora led 15,000 soldiers out of Genoa to head toward Balaclava. Of those, 1,500 of them never returned. Even here, there was little glory and honor despite the rhetoric. The Battle of Chernaya, which gave its name to numerous streets and piazzas, was merely a Scaramouche. Our soldiers died due to cholera and smallpox that decimated both the Piedmontese and allied troops. It was so cold in those desolate lands that the soldiers' feet froze in their shoes and men died without even realizing it.[43]

Cavour boasted that with that participation they could now sit for the peace discussions and could bring up the problem of Italy's oppression by foreigners. In other words, he climbed upon a mountain of corpses in order to be able to give a speech.

---

[41] R. Edgerton, *Gloria o morte* (Milan, 1999).
[42] D. Mack Smith, *Cavour; il grande tessitore dell'unità d'Italia* (Milan, 1985).
[43] A. Calani, *Scena della vita militare in Crimea* (Naples, 1855).

In any event, that expedition was to be funded with money that the Savoy State did not possess.

Another negotiation was necessary with more bankers to secure another loan.

Initially, Cavour concluded that 25 million lira would be sufficient. The English retained that that sum was greater than what was needed. Too optimistic. In October, the Piedmontese government was obliged to ask for money yet again: another 25 million. On the occasion of another mission in Great Britain, in December, he asked for money a third time: another 25 million.

Piedmont's expansionist goals, was quickly becoming a bottomless pit.

In view of the Second War of Independence (1859), more loans were requested: first for 40 million lira and then 150 million.

The Chamber of Deputies only offered 23 votes in opposition.[44] Since the money was not theirs, the members of Parliament didn't seem to pay it much attention.

Barely stopping to take a breath, we yet again found ourselves in the condition to rack up some more debt. Garibaldi (1860) had "conquered" the Kingdom of the Two Sicilies and his efforts required compensation.

The Red Shirts were, for the most part, fiercely anticlerical. Amongst the many doctrines of the Church that they chose to ignore, the most ignored was the seventh commandment: do not steal.

"The ease with which public funds were used to gratify supporters and friends should be cause for reflection on the dictatorship's management of finances. We are speaking of large sums of money that have been managed with complete autonomy and never properly reported. A significant portion of Bourbon silver had been stored in the Kingdom of Naples' vaults... millions of ducats worth of silver that simply disappeared without a trace." A great many funds were deposited between Naples and Sicily. These funds made their way to the North, France, and

---

[44] *Atti parlamentari*, 1854-1855.

England through maritime rentals and acquisitions, weapons, and clothing. Millions were lost along the way. A total of 60,000 coats were purchased for 21,000 soldiers. The excess was immediately sold on the black market. Many of Garibaldi's soldiers left their homes in tatters and returned with their pockets full of money. What was not stolen was squandered through negligence and carelessness.

The historian Roberto Martucci[45] calculated the value of the spoils: the equivalent of half a billion Piedmontese lira at the time. This is the equivalent of the future public debt of Unified Italy. This equals nine times the amount of debt accumulated by our participation in the Crimean War.

Cavour used official and secret funds to buy off sections of the Bourbon army and the admirals of the marines. He spent and favored spending absurd amounts to favor rebellions in favor of Victor Emanuel II that never reached their destinations.

In the trenches below the walls of Gaeta under siege, Goritte,[46] a lawyer presented himself before Farini, sustaining that he could convince the King of the Two Sicilies to surrender. In exchange, a part of the treasure that he had abandoned in Naples would be returned to him. This proposal was somewhat absurd considering Francis II had left that treasure behind in order to demonstrate that he did not care about the treasure. If he had only wanted, he could have requested these funds from the bank. But Count Cavour, ever informed, quickly communicated his favorable opinion by stating, "Bridges of gold to Francesco II… the fall of Gaeta will never sufficiently be paid for…."

Goritte received a large some of clandestine funds which he spent to no avail. Therefore, he requested more funds though this time the Piedmontese did not fall for his tricks. He tried to invent explanations and attempted to justify his diplomatic efforts and even attempted to be reimbursed for expenses he claimed to have already incurred. At the end

---

[45] R. Martucci, *L'invenzione dell'Italia unita 1855-1864* (Milan, 1999).
[46] P.A. Jaeger, *Francesco II di Barbone, l'ultimo re di Napoli* (Milan, 1982).

of the war, he felt morally obliged to explain everything by writing it in a book that he entitled: "A Political Attempt in December of 1860 to cede Gaeta without Further Bloodshed." This is exactly what we wanted to know.

Unfortunately, the author believed that his story would not be well understood without an introduction that established a context. It was to be a sort of preface and he began recounting the history of the Bourbon reign starting from the Restoration. The introduction became quite lengthy and began to address dynastic issues. It wound up occupying two tomes that comprised some thousand pages and weighed several kilos. Goritte did not live long enough to finish his literary masterpiece and therefore never quite managed to explain what role he had played and what the Piedmontese had done at the feet of Gaeta.

These pages were infamous. It seemed as though anyone could ask for money at his/her will.

Agostino Bertani withdrew an enormous amount of money to support the Republican Left.[47] Before the Risorgimento, he was in the medical field. His visits warranted a compensation of a franc and 30 cents each. After the Unification of Italy, "…his fortune was not less than 14 million lira, the provenance of which is unknown. Four of those millions can be somewhat traced, but the origins of these too are not the purest."[48]

Scialoja, who was quickly sent by Cavour to oversee Garibaldi's efforts, stated: "What? Do you want to make all of the millions disappear so that the only thing left is Unity?"[49]

Ippolito Nievo was one of the treasurers of the expedition, and perhaps the only honest one at that. He had kept records and balances of everything in order. When rumors that in the South there was too much plundering emerged, he sent a telegraph to Turin stating that he would have returned with all of the documents necessary to preserve his honor.

---

[47] R. Martucci, *L'invenzione dell'Italia unita 1855-1864* (Milan, 1999).

[48] E. Bianchini Braglia, *Le radici della vergogna. Psicanalisi dell'Italia* (Reggio Emilia-Modena, 2009).

[49] R. Martucci, *L'invenzione dell'Italia unita 1855-1864* (Milan, 1999).

He boarded the ship *Ercole* and never reached his destination. They noticed that the steamship was running late after a week and only then did they proceed to send out a search party. Those who believe that this was a crime committed by the State[50] have reason to spare.

Poor government knows no limits.

In 1861, sums were drawn[51] to determine the cost of the Unification of Italy (though Venice and Rome had not yet been annexed) the Minister of the Treasury, Pietro Bastogi, added up all of the deficits of the pre-Unification states. He revealed that the hole in the balance amounted to 2 billion 402 million lira. The Piedmontese debt accounted for 55% of the total mostly due to the loans taken to build the new Italy.

In this context, there is a detail that is often forgotten or hidden in the pages of history. Yet it is one of those details that says much about our DNA and on the efforts we must make to break from our past. It is only in telling ourselves the truth that we can find the motivation to redeem ourselves from our errors and transform them into little virtues.

Amongst the many debts that remained unpaid, there were obviously those incurred by the former Grand Duke of Tuscany, Leopold. He requested a loan to finance the suppression of the *Carbonari* uprising in 1848 (the one with Guerrazzi and Montanelli). That money came from the Bastogi family who guaranteed those funds with an official bank guarantee. [52] At the dawn of the formation of a new State that proposed itself before Europe and the rest of the world, there was a minister with the hands and face of a liberal, Risorgimento and Unification supporter that paid to that very same minister who in turn received that payment with the hands and face of a reactionary, obscurantist, conservative.

---

[50] S. Nievo, *Il prato in fondo al mare* (Milan, 1974).
[51] F.S. Nitti, *Il bilancio dello Stato dal 1862 al 1896-1897* (Bari, 1958).
[52] S. Turone, *Gli scandali dall'unità d'Italia alla P2* (Bari, 1980).

CHAPTER 4

PAYING TO EAT... PAYING TO BREATHE...

Around 1861, public spending was around 900 million lira and two heavy contributors to this number were the weapons and salaries for the army. The first financial act of the newly formed Italian State was to request a loan for 500 million lira. From that moment onward, the deficit continued to be covered up by the massive debts incurred by the State. When Rome was finally conquered, the last piece of the Unification puzzle, those 2.5 billion lira became 9 billion.[53]

There was nothing left. The only things left in abundance were taxes and duties that ranged from 42 to 48 percent. A tax was levied on ground meat, and this was an unfair tax because it touched the poorest citizens, and therefore the weakest members of the population. It was still not enough. Taxes were levied on windows, as was done in England. To be honest, London had already abolished this tax because the citizens that could not afford to pay this tax walled off the windows of their homes. The result was turning their homes into windowless hovels that made their inhabitants sick. Over the course of a few years, half of the population had holes in their lungs. The Parliament in Rome believed that this tax would generate a good amount of revenue for the treasury. It was a distant relative of the IMU tax.[54]

People were paying to eat and breathe.

Much like in Great Britain several years prior, those who could not or chose not to pay walled their windows shut. They drew fabulous land-

---

[53] F.S. Nitti, *Il bilancio dello Stato dal 1862 al 1896-1897* (Bari, 1958).
[54] *Editors' note*: IMU stands for "Imposta Municipale Unica," which translates into English as Local Property Tax.

scapes on these walls. The extraordinary *trompe l'œil* frescoes that can be found today prevalently in the South and in Genoa are the result of the citizens' reaction to these late nineteenth-century taxes.

They eluded themselves into believing that they could control the debt by "stealing the bread of the people by taxing their 600 lira salary while leaving the entertainment expenses incurred by the prefects intact. On the occasion of great feast days or parties, the prefects use these funds to prompt the aristocrats to dance. Well they can very well dance in the comfort of their own homes…"

Any attempt to curb this type of "joyous" spending failed miserably. When Minister Quintino Sella proposed to establish some rules to ensure the efficiency of the administration, Francesco Crispi exclaimed: "If you are proposing such reforms then you are a man with no principles!"

Giacinto De Sivo,[55] a Bourbon monarchy supporter to his core, commented: "Over the course of five years, the taxes tripled but the earth did not triple its fruits."

The race to cover expenses and the increase in taxes has continued over the course of the past 150 years without one ever catching up to the other. Certainly the money earned by the regions, towns, government entities, and the citizens would never be enough to cover the irrational expenses incurred by the Parliament's careless decisions.

Several investigations conducted by journalists have brought to light numerous bizarre expenses.

The city of Perugia has hired 13 people whose job requires them to check house numbers.[56] The autonomous province of Bolzano has activated courses of all sorts: for the conservation of cheese, on anti-noise barriers, on bon-ton, and on "how to say 'yes' to a 'no'."[57]

Sicily has hired "runners" who go from office to office with documents, though in this modern age, one can send them via computer by simply

---

[55] G. De Sivo, *Storia delle Due Sicilie dal 1847 al 1861* (Rome, 1863-1864).
[56] M. Giordano, *Spudorati. La grande beffa dei costi della politica: false promesse e verità nascoste* (Milan, 2012).
[57] Ibid.

pushing a button.[58] Always in Sicily, 4,800 euro went to the guitar instructor of the town Barcellona Pozzo di Gotto. Another 22,000 euro were needed to "monitor the organizational processes relating to the institutional relations between the region and the State". One might rightly say what the money was actually allotted for is not clearly discernible from the given explanation. The only thing that is comprehensible is that 100 euro per day were spent.[59] Then there are the 200 million euro that were spent in 1984 for the purchase of two Icelandic orca whales which were destined for an aquarium along the coast of Sciacca. In reality, the structure was never built, so it would appear that those whales were taken care of in their own waters at our expense.[60]

In Florence, 13,000 euro were required in order to count the city's bicycle racks.[61] Professor Cristiano Celone greatly applied himself to study the "design and implementation of policies for development, with particular attention to external conditions."[62] The region of Sardinia required a humidity expert in order to "elaborate data regarding the birds" in a given area. In Umbria, instead, three experts were required to "monitor the genetics of the wolf population."[63]

The province of Treviso spent 21,000 euro to count eels.[64] The Friuli-Venezia-Giulia region destined 26,370 euro of its funds to "formulate contracts to hire experts qualified to determine whether it is snowing."[65]

---

[58] M. Feltri, "Spese folli in Sicilia. La Regione assume i "camminatori". Avranno il compito di 'trasferire documenti'" *La Stampa*, May 17, 2012.

[59] M. Giordano, *Spudorati. La grande beffa dei costi della politica: false promesse e verità nascoste* (Milan, 2012).

[60] G. Villa, "Dai 30 mila forestali all'assegno per le orche: l'antologia della spreco. Tutti i record negativi della Regione sull'orlo del baratro: ai consiglieri uno stipendio da senatore con rimborsi doppi" in *Il Giornale*, July 19, 2012.

[61] M. Giordano, *Spudorati. La grande beffa dei costi della politica.*

[62] Ibid.

[63] Ibid.

[64] MIC, "Nord Est sprecone, soldi pubblici per guardare se nevica. La provincia di Treviso conta le anguille. Nel Padovano 'aiutini' agli spaventapasseri" in *Il Giornale*, April 3, 2012.

[65] Ibid.

In the town of Grantorto, near Padua, 400 euro were allotted to the "scarecrow laboratory."[66]

The television program *Le Iene* discovered that taxpayer money was used to fund the penitentiary police's soccer team. In 2010 and 2011, two public contests were held for 12 positions on the soccer team with a long term contract on the A.S. Astrea team. This team plays in Series D and is headed by the penitentiary administration. In the contract with the ministry, once a player retires, they are entitled to a desk job in another office. At the moment of the scandal, the Minister of Justice Paola Severino assured[67] that this would all come to an end. But it is still going on....

In 2012, the Chamber of Deputies spent 398,172 euro for toner, it purchased 10,531 euro worth of flags, and spent 56,725 euro for wardrobe expenses. The press office cost 3,100,000 euro while the library cost 2,920,000 euro. In order to purchase adequate software, 4,800,000 euro were spent including 2.5 million euro for maintenance.[68]

But there is not enough money to pay for all of these expenses....

To be honest, we no longer have the money to fund the huge projects where Italy showcases its grandeur. If Mrs. Merkel, as it seems, expects that our balance will quickly even itself out then we should start by saving on international missions. Perhaps she and her country should represent us in Afghanistan, Iraq, the Balkans, Syria, Palestine, and in the rest of the world where we are present with extremely costly peace missions. She and her very wealthy country should invest in matters of international security so that we can begin saving in order to lower our level of public debt and embark upon a cycle of virtue. Europe and Germany cannot request commitments that are always more pressing and expensive

---

[66] Ibid.

[67] M. Gorra, "La ministra promette: basta soldi per i calciatori. Sull'incredibile squadra della Polizia penitenziaria la Severino dà ragione a *Libero*: 'Interverrò, non dobbiamo usare fondi pubblici. Copriremo i costi con gli sponsor'" in *Libero*, April 20, 2012.

[68] M. Giordano, "La Camera si pappa 20 mila euro di dolci. Scoop di Tgcom 24 che ha recuperato le singole voci di spesa per la gestione dei Deputati" in *Libero*, January 19, 2013.

when it comes to collective initiatives and then chastise us in private when it comes time for us to justify a deficit. This deficit was also brought about by their decisions. They cannot ask us to take care of serious matters, especially when we throw money out. In the name of the program "Humanitarian mission for the stabilization and reconstruction of Iraq" (the slogan for the "Ancient Babylon" mission) we offered the IPALMO organization 269,000 Euro to facilitate the "dialog amongst Iraqis." The ONG organization spearheaded by Emma Bonino received 381,000 for a project that "aims to create a cultural-political dialog with the objective of creating a space where people can speak in a free and open manner". Landau received 98,000 for a "round table discussion on the international situation." Then 349,000 euro and change went to Minerva to finance a 6 day trip to 3 Iraqi cities for a few artists: a singer, a small orchestra, and a writer. Minerva also received another 301,000 euro for a "project to create a sociopolitical analysis on the problem of human trafficking." Many humanitarian organizations came forth to promote some initiative: this amount comes to 4 million euro[69].

It is no longer the time for us to have two aircraft carriers.

The *Garibaldi* should be sent to a junkyard.

The *Cavour* does not work. It was ordered and inaugurated with much fanfare and horns along with the presence of then President Carlo Azeglio Ciampi. Judging from what experts have had to say about it, it is a lemon. The *Cavour* does not have a bridge for horizontal takeoffs therefore it holds twenty or so Harrier planes that can take off vertically. These planes are, however, soon to be obsolete. Therefore, they are awaiting the arrival of the new F-35 planes of which one hundred or so have been ordered. However, the prototypes have not been satisfying and they are constantly being redesigned and updated. Nevertheless, they seem to be scrap metal. The *Cavour* runs the serious risk of being downgraded from being classified as an aircraft carrier to a helicopter carrier. It costs

---

[69] F. Bechis, "Concerti, cene e formazione delle toghe: per ricostruire l'Iraq buttiamo 4 milioni" in *Libero*, November 29, 2012.

us 100,000 euro a day when it sits in the port and 200,000 euro when it sails.[70] It was sent to Haiti when the island was hit by the earthquake and it was used as a hospital. Even in a situation such as that, a beautiful ship such as the *Cavour* was unnecessary: any old ship that stayed afloat as holding areas would have sufficed.

We no longer have the money to pay for electoral reimbursements that in Italy cost 25 times more than in other European countries.[71] We no longer have the money to pay for the salaries of those members of Parliament, whose incomes are higher than any other government member on the planet. We no longer have the money to pay for the thermal bath cures[72] of ministers nor for the chauffeured car service offered to former presidents who were in office ten years ago.

How much effort is really needed to curb our expenses and to restore some order by removing even only a few of the government's privileges? When it comes to taxing citizens, the laws are passed in a heartbeat and are retroactive. If the laws regard Parliament, they take forever to pass (if they pass) and take forever to go into effect.

Someone actually hoped that the provisory government would be able to proceed with more speed by avoiding some of the obstacles that have challenged its predecessors, which were always a bit shaky and subject to the instability of the majority party.

There was nothing to be done. Even the professors lacked the courage necessary to take action.

What? The premise, though not demonstrated, was treated as though it were a consolidated fact, was that we were in a terrible state. There-

---

[70] P. Granzotto, 'Piaccia o non piaccia, la portaerei Cavour costa davvero troppo" in *Il Giornale*, May 8, 2012.

[71] P. Bracalini, "Rimborsi elettorali Italia sprecona. Londra spende 25 volte meno. In Inghilterra la spesa annuale è 12 milioni mentre da noi 289. In Spagna un tetto a 82 milioni" in *Il Giornale*, April 10, 2012.

[72] F. Bechis, "Ai deputati terme e massaggi pagati. L'assistenza integrativa di Montecitorio prevede anche fanghi, elettroscultura e shiatsu terapia fino a un tetto di 1.860 euro all'anno per ogni onorevole. Tutto grazie a una convenzione stipulata con un centro privato a due passi dal parlamento" in *Libera*, April 20, 2012.

fore, emergency for emergency, we required a government with 10 ministers (which we could not do without) and 2 more for the economy. In this moment of extraordinary chaos, what need would we have for a Minister for Territorial Cohesion? Why would we need a Minister for International Cooperation?

The members of the "technical" government arrived asking for blood and tears but it is quite evident that those sacrifices needed to be distributed in equal parts. One should at least pretend that they are making an effort. For example, if the newly appointed ministers had decided to leave—oh, I don't know—say 30% or 40% of their salaries in the coffers of the State then perhaps the tax increase that they proposed would seem as though it were a painful but unavoidable necessity. Besides, for a lawyer with an income of 7 million euro per year and a banker who declared to make just below that income as well, would it really have been such a big sacrifice? It would have been a small one that would have had a huge psychological impact. It would also have been a good starting point to ask the members of Parliament to do the same. I would have really enjoyed seeing how Fini and Schifani would have scrambled to try to ensure that an analogous measure did not pass.

The members of the provisory government began with all of the best intentions, sobriety, and composure. However, in the end, they only took on the burden of levying taxes with an authoritarian air that was socially ill-accepted.

Who knows how they reacted to the news of a retired woman from Gela throwing herself from a balcony because she didn't believe she could afford to live. She had an 800-euro pension and they reduced it 200 euro.[73]

Were super-experts who graduated from the Bocconi University necessary to take the people's savings? With bitterness, the secretary of the

---

[73] L. Scime, "Con l'incubo di non farcela si lancia dal balcone. Un'anziana di Gela si era trovata con la pensione decurtata da 800 a 600 euro" in *la Repubblica*, April 3, 2012.

CISL (the Italian Workers' Union) Raffaele Bonanni[74] commented, "my uncle could have pulled off that maneuver." Let us say the truth: which of us does not have an uncle in the family who would be so bold as to go around asking for money in that manner?

Now they boast of the pension reform as though it were something new and innovative. In reality, Berlusconi's first term in 1994 had already decided that this issue needed to be addressed, though perhaps in a timelier manner and without the necessary discussions. The result was that the piazzas quickly filled with protesters. Berlusconi returned to power in 2001 with a proposal that was a little less harsh: those who were at the retirement age could continue to work without having to pay a tax on their salary. The worker could therefore have a salary 30% higher than a pension, and the employer would not have to pay that 30% to social security. In addition, social security would not have to dispense a pension. It seemed to be the perfect solution to everyone's problems. As soon as Prodi was elected into office, the first law he abolished was that one.

So the only thing that the provisory government managed to do was to levy taxes that brought the Italians to their knees. It is similar to when a donkey can no longer continue walking because he is too heavily burdened.

So what's the latest tax? In Borgo San Dalmazzo, in the province of Cuneo, if one chooses to keep the ashes of a cremated loved one, a 48-euro tax must be paid.[75] A tax levied on the dead. The revenue office does not even spare you once you die.

The economists from the Bocconi praise these various tax maneuvers and Europe applauds us for our newly acquired austerity and re-established authority. Nevertheless, neither of these manages to fill the bellies of the common folk. The vast majority of the people don't have a euro to spare. Carlo Cerofolini, a journalist writing for the newspaper *Il*

---

[74] REOL, "Il giorno dello sciopero per il pubblico impiego. Scontro per l'articolo 18. A Roma invasa piazza Montecitorio" in *Corriere della Sera*, December 19, 2012.
[75] Na. Mur., "Siamo il paese del balzelli: ci tocca pure pagare la tassa sui morti" in *Il Giornale*, December 19, 2012.

Giornale, painted a very grim picture of our situation: "GDP -2.3, unemployment 10.6, deficit/GDP -2.9, debt/GDP 126.5 (or 2 billion euro), interest expenses/GDP 5.4, private consumption -3.4, consumer's trust has gone down from 96 to 86, internal demand -5%, interest rates 4.8, fiscal oppression/GDP 55, non-performing loans 116 billion euro, and so continues the disaster."[76]

The Bank of Italy, according to Ignazio Visco its governor, confirmed that the recession will continue to bite. In 2013, the GDP fell by another point and the unemployment rate sky rocketed to 12 points.[77]

The President of the Court of Auditors Luigi Giampaolino, in his 2012 report, could not avoid stating that "too many taxes produce recessive impulses" which risk creating "a downward spiral." Even according to him "there are no more margins that would allow us to increase withdrawals"[78] from the pockets of the citizens.

The "authority" known as the *Financial Times*[79] published an article entitled: "Monti is not the right man for Italy." In their opinion, he is comparable to Heinrich Brüning, the German Chancellor who from 1930 to 1932 implemented harsh and useless economic policies that ultimately paved the way for Adolf Hitler's dictatorship.

Aside from drawing parallels, Italy is paying an exorbitant amount of taxes without receiving adequate services. The Italian internal revenue office is as greedy as its German counterpart but is as inefficient as that of an African state.

---

[76] C. Cerofolini, "Lettere al Direttore. Un anno di disastri. Chi vuole un Monti bis guardi prima i numeri" in *Il Giornale*, November 25, 2012.

[77] S. Tamburello, "'Recessione nel 2013'. Bankitalia: Pil in calo dell'uno per cento. Visco contestato all'Università di Firenze" in *Corriere della Sera*, January 19, 2013.

[78] G. Franzese, "La Corte dei Conti: troppe tasse e corruzione frenano la crescita. Il presidente Giampaolino avverte: esauriti i margini per aumentare il prelievo. L'Italia rischia di avvitarsi e restare intrappolata in un circolo vizioso" in *Il Messaggero*, June 6, 2012.

[79] W. Munchau, "Perché Monti non è la persona giusta per l'Italia" in *Financial Times*, January 21, 2013.

Piero Ostellino noted "in those places where the withdrawal surpasses, as is our case, certain percentage levels of the wealth produced and the incomes received by workers, and therefore distinguishes itself as a confiscation rather than the basis of a welfare system, the question as to whether it shouldn't be the State supplying a justification regarding its 'unjust' laws, and not the citizen justifying their violation, is a legitimate one and the answer on the part of the State is only fair."[80]

What is the last resort? The fight against tax evasion would allow for the collection of a mountain of billions of tax euro that are currently dispersed in a black hole that is currently out of the government's control. Is it possible? How is it that over the course of the past few decades we have not managed, I am not even saying "eliminate," but to at least limit this grey area?

The truth is that the average honest citizen, in most cases, is an accomplice to tax evasion, and actually encourages it. Let us pretend that we are an average family with a "husband" that earns 1,500 euro a month and a "wife" that contributes another 1,000 euro. In these times, that isn't even so bad, but once they pay the rent, send their child or children to school, pay the heating bill, buy groceries, buy a coat, and pay the other bills, there is little money left. Say they have to go to a dentist who charges a fee of around 8 to 12,000 euro (dentists here does not charge less) and when his work is done, he offers the family the opportunity to either pay the bill with the IVA tax or pay up front in cash with a considerable discount. That 30% difference does not represent wealth to our hypothetical family, but survival. Which choice is more convenient for that family? If they come to terms and illegally pay the dentist without receiving a bill it is not to commit fraud, earn money, or enrich themselves. They are not bad people, but they do not have that kind of money in their wallets. The State has already taken that money from their salaries before it has even reached their wallet.

---

[80] P. Ostellino, "L'esosità del fisco e le domande dei cittadini. Lo Stato è obbligato a giustificare un prelievo fiscale eccessivo" in *Corriere della Sera*, December 5, 2012.

The same thing happens when the plumbing in the bathroom breaks. How are they supposed to behave with the plumber? What happens when the roof needs repairs? How are they supposed to behave with the workers? It is no coincidence that dentists, plumbers, and bricklayers are at the top of the list of the worst (presumed) tax evaders.

So what is the solution? All we have to do is look around us and copy what we see. What happens in the rest of the world, where things actually work? The families present their balance, just like businesses do, with credits and debits along with the final gains. The taxes are paid upon the net gains and therefore everyone has a common interest in saving every receipt, including the ones for the occasional espresso. If the internal revenue office is dishonest (as it is now) it will ask you for 50% but it will be 50% from your final gains, in other words one's savings. As it stands now, the government takes 50% of the gross amount, in other words what one would collect, and with the other half one is supposed to live and pay for family expenses, while making sacrifices such as requesting no receipt so as to avoid paying the IVA tax.

If families were to present their balances like businesses we could shut down *Equitalia*, the majority of the tax offices, and there would be no need for audits or for the Financial Police. Mothers and wives would become the revenue officers of their own homes: not one receipt would escape their eagle eyes! Everyone would pay their taxes and the State would save money on some 10,000 salaries of those auditors, some of which are quite generous. At that point, the iron-clad "zero tolerance" rule for tax evasion would be justified.

Part III

Greedy Hands and Guilty Consciences

CHAPTER 1

FIRST, MAZZINI'S BRIBE THEN THE PLEBISCITE FOR THE UNIFICATION OF ITALY

"I can only say that while others would attempt to make any business endeavor their own, he aims to fill the Coffers of the party and not his own."[1] He wrote coffer with a capital "C" in order to provide an air of dignity to his request for illegal funding. Black on white, this letter was written and signed on Giuseppe Mazzini's own stationery: that very same Mazzini who was wanted by the police of half the countries in Europe. He had some difficulty personally attending meetings but he could still direct any discussion held due to the many friendships he had and could also count on the prestige that comes with being one of the country's Founding Fathers.

The message was addressed to Francesco Crispi who, before becoming a staunch advocate of the monarch and practicing a reactionary sort of politics, had previously broken bread with the radical Left.

The message was only a few lines long and written by hand with a slightly pointy penmanship. With all of the evidence available and some hindsight, the contents of this note appear to be compromising. However, at the very least he did not pretend to hide behind too many florid words. "Brother," he wrote, "the carrier of this letter is Adriano Lemmi. He has been a dear friend for over twenty years and has made considerable sacrifices for the Cause." He wrote the word cause with a capital "C" to confer an idealistic tone to the vulgarity that he was proposing. "He comes to speak of a very important matter concerning the railways. I beg

---

[1] V. Di Nardo, *Oh, mia Patria. Un inviato speciale nel primo anno dell'unità d'Italia* (Milan, 1990).

you to listen to him: he will explain all."[2] He wanted the contract to build the railway that would connect the North to the South by train.

Garibaldi had just arrived in Naples. He had declared the dynasty of the Bourbon monarchs to be over and had personally assumed the role of a dictator. Not for himself, the supporters of the Risorgimento want to specify, but in the name of Victor Emanuel II of Savoy. He wanted to give a bit of a democratic flair to an international aggression that occurred with no justifications and a war of conquest that was conducted without shame. He expected to obtain the approval of the public and called for a referendum that he called a "plebiscite" so that it would be clear from the very beginning that the final result should be plebiscitary: unanimous. The predicted and convincing consensus from the public should have been sufficient to sway the public opinion of the rest of Europe's capitals that the attack of the Red Shirts on the Kingdom of the Two Sicilies was justifiable.

Garbaldi was welcomed triumphantly into Naples on September 7th. The plebiscite took place on October 21st. Mazzini's letter does not have a date but can certainly be estimated to have been written within these 45 days.

Therefore Italy did not formally exist. The Unification, on a legal level, was non-existent and, in order to become effective, still required another vote. Yet there were already requests for bribes and the promise of illegal funding for political parties.

Our troubles began at precisely that moment. Hiding this truth, minimizing it or, even worse, distorting is of no help to those who study history and is damaging to the country. This is because history teaches us about life. It teaches us not to repeat the same mistakes and to improve ourselves and our people. If we replace the truth with fairy tales that are loaded with noble sentiments then we have nothing left to learn. Rhetoric may warm the heart but it does not allow us to use our reasoning.

---

[2] Ibid.

By consulting the pages of history, it would seem as though for a hundred years Italy's governing class has been the incarnation of morality.

They were honest, romantic, devout, altruistic, inspired to do the best for the common good, thousands of miles away from catering to their own personal needs. They were all Fathers of the Country and worthy of being placed on bronze pedestals so that future generations might admire them. All of them were, including Alcide De Gasperi.

Then all of a sudden they became news features. We discovered that they were thieves and that some of them stole a great deal.

How is this possible? From whom could they have learned?

Perhaps some controversial research destroyed a few myths of which we had become fond, but this at least allows us to comprehend our real past. This alone is the key to understanding our present and to help plan our future with some hope of success.

The thieves present at the dawn of that first monarchy were the great-grandfathers and great-great grandfathers of the thieves of the First Republic. Their methods are the same. They have the same imprint and the same carelessness. Sometimes, from one century to the next, their last names may recur. Other times, it is their uncanny resemblance that resurfaces. The things that remain the same are the projects, their bold faces, and their presumptuous conviction that they will get away with their crime.

In September of 1860, Garibaldi formed a new government and called his most trusted men, many of whom fought alongside him as one of the *Mille*, to his side. Francesco Crispi was his right-hand man. At this point they needed to take care of ordinary administration tasks, but anyone who assumes that the Ministers assigned to handle the various ministries would only take care of those business matters would be sadly mistaken. There were also strategic matters to manage that needed to be steered towards the most convenient solutions.

The communication issue was considered a very important problem. The new country, which spanned 1,200 kilometers, was in dire need of transportation to link its cities. At the time, the only way to connect these cities and towns was through an adequate railway system. Historians barely addressed this issue. The little attention they paid was dedicated to mocking the Bourbon monarchs who inaugurated their own railroad in 1839. Allegedly this railway was a joke to the royal family who enjoyed riding the train from Naples to Portici. Cavour, on the other hand, with his farsighted politics during the "decade of preparation" had invested a consistent portion of the budget to give Piedmont a modern network of railways. This would have been useful, in particular, for the transportation of goods.

According to the traditional vulgate, on one hand we have a bunch of do-nothing aristocrats from the South, who were attracted by the novelty of such technology as children to an amusement park, and on the other the efficient entrepreneurs of the North who were capable of predicting the evolution of the markets and therefore able to adapt to the changes in a timely manner.

In reality, this was not the case. The trains in the North operated thanks to the initiative taken by the Austrian government, while the South had already planned for an expansion of its railway network. It was to develop two new branches. On the Eastern side, the trains would have left from Brindisi and would have reached Pescara before proceeding onward to Ancona and Bologna. On the other side, Calabria would have been connected to Rome and would have then proceeded along the Tyrrhenian Coast to Florence, Genoa, and Turin. Some routes had already been built and some cities and towns were already linked: Torre del Greco, Castellammare di Stabia, Capua, and Sparanise. One could even reach Salerno and Caserta. Even at this pace, the expansion would have taken a long time to complete.

It is for this reason that the Bourbon monarchs issued an international contest to encourage foreign participation in helping them to expand their railways system as quickly as possible. Before Garibaldi's invasion, the contracts had already been assigned to a family of French bankers: the Talabot family. They had perfected their project and had already informed the monarchs that they were ready to commence building.

The war prevented the executive phase of those projects and solutions. However, the new government in Naples, though it was still a provisory one, decided to involve themselves in the matter. This decision roused a great deal of interest.

Adriano Lemmi was quick to arrive on the scene with the letter of recommendation signed by Mazzini that should have settled the matter.

How could one ignore the request of the "apostle of thought and action"? Nevertheless, it was not easy to meet all of his requests.

Pietro Augusto Adami, a Tuscan banker, was also quick to request a meeting with Giuseppe Garibaldi. He boasted of the funds he was able to obtain to financially support the *Mille* in their efforts and now claimed the rightful compensation due to a "disinterested patriot"[3].

There was one contract and two contenders. Garibaldi and Crispi arranged for a meeting in order to make a decision. We are not privy to the details of that meeting or the passion with which each of them supported their respective contenders. The result, however, was equal: half of the contract was to go to Adami and the other half was assigned to Lemmi. In the end, the two gentlemen were brothers-in-law and, in the past, had no problems handling such agreements.

The new railways were a colossal task. It would be necessary to build a network of 6,000 kilometers worth of tracks. They would also have to allot 210 million lira for the purchase of lands, the setup of the foundation, and the hardware. Another 30 million lira would be necessary to purchase mobile material, the stations, and the tolls. Next, one needed to think about hiring the managers, workers, technicians, and engineers. All in all, this required a budget of around 1.5 billion lira at the time, 1861. This was not an easy task because the professionals required to first, design and then manage the development of such a railway system could be counted on one hand.

In any event, the budget was a frighteningly large one for those times, and the salaries to be earned were divided proportionately. The winners

---

[3] V. Di Nardo, *Oh, mia Patria.*

of the contract, once they had made their calculations, decided that they had just made the deal of their lives. They decided that they needed to put forth at least a portion of the bribe that they had promised. This money served to finance the *"Popolo d'Italia"* newspaper that would be printed in Naples.[4] It was to have Pro-Republic leanings but without using an exasperating tone when addressing the current reigning Monarchy.

However, it is one matter to obtain a contract and quite another to carry out the project. One required building yards and structures that the two bankers did not have and did not manage to procure. The Tuscan duo was forced to withdraw from the contract. The new Italy was forced to spend a few million lira to hire consultants, perform inspections, place payments, request estimates, perform topographical surveys and geographical analyses. Having done all of these things, they still managed not to build even a meter of the prospected railway system. What to do next?

The government, using the technique of belated apologies and the diplomatic technique of "a thousand promises" attempted to contact the Talabot family; however they no longer wanted to participate. A solution appeared to be close at hand when in the spring of 1862, the Ministry of Labor received an offer for the contract of the South's railways. They had piqued the interest of James Rothschild, one of the richest men in the world and the heir to a family that had been a member of "high society" on both sides of the ocean for many generations. The proposal was an advantageous one and after all of the time that had been wasted, it did not seem wise to dawdle and delay action any further. On the 15th of June, with unusual speed, and off-the-record indiscretions confirmed (though they were legitimized by the authority of the sources) the Council of Ministers assured that the decision would be favorable to Rothschild's obtaining the contract. Certainly the approval of the Parliament was still required, but this was to be a mere formality. There was no reason to believe that the representatives would have differing opinions from

---

[4] M. Costa Cardol, *Ingovernabili da Torino. I tormentati esordi dell'unità d'Italia* (Milan, 1989).

the Council. Instead, that offer was thrown into the trash can faster than it could have been approved.

There were no explanations offered but there were definitely reasons that determined this decision.

So what happened? There was much money involved that could allow one to imagine garnering hefty profits from such a contract. Why should a foreign investor be favored?

Pietro Bastrogi, a representative and minister, but most importantly an entrepreneur, intervened. In a handful of days, without bothering to think too much about any conflict of interest, he managed to put together a company that stepped in and placed a bid for the construction of the South's railways. A base capital of 100 million lira was deposited and all of the shareholders were Italian. As far as the projects were concerned, three sub-contracts were issued: Credito mobiliare, the Brassery family, and a handful of Lombard entrepreneurs. These three came together to form a cooperative company.[5]

Bastogi was slated to obtain 210,000 lira for each kilometer of track laid down, as had been written in the contract, but would have only paid 198,000. Any profit would have been divided into two parts: half to Bastogi and the other half was to be divided further into fifths to the sub-contractors and any number of other people gravitating around that tangled mass of companies and interests. In the end, it was an idea that came out of nowhere but those who came up with it managed to effortlessly earn a sizeable sum of money and guarantee a salary to all those who carried out the job, essentially parasites of the mediation effort.[6] The Bastogi family hailed from the town of Civitavecchia but had since moved to Livorno. They were considered nobles and undoubtedly were the ones who would have received the greatest benefit from this contract without risking much of anything. Even in the past, their opportunism allowed them

---

[5] S. Turone, *Gli scandali dall'unità d'Italia alla P2* (Bari, 1980).
[6] Ibid.

to accumulate wealth and had allowed them safe passage even through the many government upsets.

The Parliament, without too much thought and actually with a great deal of genuine enthusiasm, approved the banker from Livorno's proposal. They did not even try to keep up appearances. No one bothered to notice that in the list of associates many names were actually repeated and that there were many inaccuracies that would have warranted further analysis upon how this company was actually founded. No technical objections were made to the procedures implemented. No one bothered to notice (or perhaps no one thought it necessary to further analyze) that the provisory address for the company's headquarters was the residence of a representative from Turin named Bartolomeo Beltrami.

The President of the Public Works Committee, the Honorable Ambrogio Terzi, presented such a favorable report that it almost seemed like an apology. The President of the Chamber, Urbano Rattazzi, in a brief moment of objective clarity, felt the need to ask, "But are you speaking on behalf of the public that has elected you or as the spokesperson for Mr. Bastogi?"[7]

A few weeks later, the board of directors of the company was nominated and of the 22 members, 14 were representatives that had been carefully chosen so that they represented important groups, families, and wealthy individuals that spanned the political spectrum. Pietro Bastogi was the president and in Parliament he represented the area of Vicopisano, near Pisa. His vice-presidents were Bettino Ricasoli and Giovanni Baracco: the former was elected in Florence and the latter was elected in Crotone (near Catanzaro). The secretary position was assigned to Guido Susani, a representative from BatogSondrio and that of the technical director was Severino Grattoni from Ceva, in the province of Cuneo.[8]

---

[7] *Atti parlamentari*, second semester 1862, sitting 11 September.

[8] The other members of the board of directors were: Ambrogio Trezzi from Milan, Antonio Allievi from Desio, Rodolfo Audinot from Vergato (Bologna), Bartolomeo Cini from Pistoia, Tommaso Corsi from San Casciano in Val di

From an economic standpoint, this operation was conducted in an entirely unbiased manner. As far as the politically ethic aspect was concerned, the operation was murky and difficult to justify.

How can one imagine that such a blatant conflict of interest did not provoke some perplexities in regards to its legitimacy?

Certainly, in an era in which the perils of a monopoly had not yet been identified an anti-trust law could not be devised. But shouldn't a little common sense on the part of the state been sufficient to see that the same people could not make the laws, pass the laws, allot funds, withdraw those same funds, spend them, present the finished work, and inspect it?

In order to make the project even more enticing, Bastogi proceeded to build a factory in Naples to produce the locomotive engines. The prototype was the distant relative of the Alfasud. The intention, as always, was to create new jobs even if the final balance was destined to include enormous invested capital and infinitesimal results.

Pesa (Florence), Cesare Valerio di Camerino (Macerata), Felice Genero, and Giacomo Filippo from Turin.

CHAPTER 2

BRIBES FOR THE REPRESENTATIVES

A few years later, and purely by chance, details emerged from this contract for the railways that led people to believe that the corruption involved was not marginal and was done with great style. Bastogi and company's contract suddenly became a scandal.

From this perspective, the diary of the lawyer from Turin, Domenico Giuriati, represents an exceptional historical document and, at the same time, a derisive glimpse into the political corruption at the time of the Savoy monarchy. Giuriati recorded a conversation held with two representatives from Tuscany.[9] One was Eugenio Pelosi, who as a university student, had harbored sympathy for Mazzini, but the government only offered seats in Parliament to those who leaned Right. This proved to be enough for him to abandon the notions of the democratic revolution and embrace the moderate doctrines of the conservatives. The other gentleman was Paolo Sinibaldi who was a commander, engineer, and a professor at the Polytechnic University of Florence.

The meeting took place in Turin, on Via Bogino, in an apartment that was small and dignified (to serve as proof that its inhabitant was not one for ostentatious displays of wealth) that Sinibaldi used when his duties as a representative required him to remain in the city. Sinibaldi was in bed due to a fever and in a state of fear of finding himself facing a number of troubles. Recently, a series of letters had surfaced written by a Vatican prelate where his name appeared regarding a violation of State secrets. This would seem like not much of a big deal but the Chamber was preparing an interrogation and the debate that would ensue could

---

[9] V. Di Nardo, *Oh, mia Patria.*

have had some serious repercussions on his political career. Pelosi wanted to meet with him to advise him to resign his position so that he would not be obliged to answer the questions he would be asked. The lawyer, Giuriati had accompanied him because, as a man of the legal profession, he could determine what the possible consequences could be on the civil, penal, and administrative levels.

Giuriati left a written testament of this encounter in his memoirs. He did not focus much on the matters regarding the letters from the Vatican, which must have seemed a matter of little importance to him due to the fact that it was not possible to reconstruct a detailed account of what actually happened. What does matter is the exchange between the gentlemen that Giuriati faithfully recorded in his writings.

"One must keep in mind," interjected Pelosi, "that the biggest mistakes one commits are not errors made from one's convictions, but those committed to care for one's own best interests...."

Sinibaldi's response was one made out of self-defense and wound up being self-accusatory. "Interests? Me?" Sinibaldi propped himself with his elbows on his mattress to straighten his back. "But if I have only ever worked like a dog and been happy with all that I have. I who have had no needs and desires...?! I, who have never been as wealthy as I am now as a university professor?! I, who thanks to God, have always had a reputation filled with such integrity and disinterest as to never fear any rival?" And, as though he were trying to reinforce his position with tangible proof, he added: "If I had not had such a sterling reputation do you really believe that I would have been offered the duty of distributing the shares of the Southern Railways to the representatives?"

Pelosi, being Tuscan, did not hesitate to ask for further explanations. "WHAT? What," he interrupted. "Certainly," repeated Sinibaldi, "I distributed them!" The confirmation came in a definitive manner and with utmost clarity. "If I had truly been money hungry," he underlined, "it would have been very easy for me to take advantage of the fact that I had been given 3 million lira to distribute to 30 representatives, don't you think?"

The lawyer intervened, "Do you realize what you are saying?" He harbored some doubt and perhaps hoped that he had misunderstood. "Are you speaking the truth?" Sinibaldi did not accept to be contradicted: "I beg that you do not doubt me." He raised his voice a little, putting pressure on his malady which irritated his throat; as if to underline the fact that there was nothing further to be said regarding the issue.

"Do you have the proof of what you are saying?"

"Certainly! I have the numbers, the names, the dates… everything… except the receipts from the notary."[10] He was forced to pronounce this last phrase with an unintentionally mocking tone. The receipts of such a bribe were clearly not signed by anyone.

Giuriati writes that the conversation "went on for a few hours" but regarding issues that, with respect to the one discussed, had little value. Shortly after taking his leave from the other two gentlemen, he did not return home and immediately went to the King's attorney, Onorato Vigilani, who was a longtime friend. Giuriati was a man of the law who was aware of details that could be considered crimes of a certain degree and he did not feel it appropriate to keep this information concealed in a compliant veil of silence. He told the magistrate the details of the conversation that he had witnessed firsthand and he proceeded to sign a written formal accusation that however, remained buried in the drawers of Justice.

In any event, the efforts made to hide this controversy did not prevent any rumors from leaking out. Some even made it to the pages of newspapers that did not support the government in power. They may have only been allusions to the actual facts but they were enough to cause more than a few ripples in the government, whose members were well informed enough to read between the lines.

The Minister Antonio Mordini from Montecatini was the first member of Parliament to bring up the matter. He was a democrat and representative of the opposing faction and he called for an investigation to

---

[10] V. Di Nardo, *Oh, mia Patria.*

shed light on this issue of the railway contracts because he believed that such rumors were damaging the government's reputation. "This fever of participating in the construction of grand public works," he observed, "this need to undertake these massive projects has prompted a lust for preposterous profits and has only served to further foster a cult of speculation. Italy, like other countries, has been infected by this plague." He made this solemn and prudent declaration in the heavy stuccos and rich velvet-clad hall that housed the seat of the government. "We must urgently proceed!" he shouted, "If we do not hurry and finish the construction of this levee soon, corruption will overflow! The most upright members of our government find their reputations called into question and in truth there are no reputations that remain intact at the moment. It has been known for some time that there are sinister rumors regarding the Southern railways that have been circulating in the newspapers. This is something we must immediately address."[11]

A good portion of the government, including the Ministers and that gentleman known as the king, would have willingly done without dealing with such a matter but faced with an official public request it would have been difficult for them to respond negatively.

The investigation committee was nominated and those appointed were chosen quite carefully so that the final result was determined before their work even commenced. Those representatives that had the most at stake were called to cover up their best interests and the only representative of the opposition, Benedetto Musolino, was rendered incapable of properly carrying out his job.

Three weeks were sufficient to clarify the matter along with a dozen page report. In this manner, on July 15, 1864 Giovanni Lanza, who was selected as the president of commission, was capable of reassuring the Chamber on the correct behavior of his colleagues. Everything was in order, except perhaps a small irregularity that could be attributed to the Honorable Guido Susani from Sondrio who, for his "services," had de-

---

[11] *Atti parlamentari*, second semester 1864, sitting of 21 July.

posited 675,000 lira from Pietro Bastogi that had been given to him from the teller at the Weiss-Norsa bank. The committee did not see the need to verify the motives behind this transfer of money or the quality of the services rendered by the representative. This type of behavior was subsequently filed under "poor personal moral conduct." Susani however, presented his resignation and moved to Paris were not too long after, he died. Some actually believed it may have been a suicide.[12]

But what happened to all of the others? The lawyer, Giuriati, was called before the investigation committee who proceeded to record his deposition. His memories, despite being lucid and detailed, were insufficient to warrant any action. He made sure that his deposition was actually filed at the public prosecutor's office of Turin and he also verified that effectively no legal action ever actually followed. They did not retain it opportune to even inform the magistrate that he had "omitted the official records." They did not even try to ask him why, according to him, the information he had received and delivered under oath was only good for the trash can.

Perhaps they would have needed the direct contribution of Sinibaldi himself who could have directly confirmed or denied any relevant information. The representative was still in a convalescent state and still was feverish from the same malady though it was brought on by another cause. But he had changed mattresses: he was no longer in his *pied-à-terre* in Turin and had returned to his noble residence in Borgo a Mozzano. He could not attend the Parliament meetings and the "grand inquisitors" spared themselves the annoyance and strife of a long trip to Lucca that would have required days of their absence and efforts that were deemed excessive.

They decided to employ bureaucratic measures instead. They picked up a pen and a piece of paper and wrote down all of the contestations and questions they had wanted to ask their colleague and were very careful as to attribute the proper respectful tone to the missive. The questions

---

[12] F. Boeri, *Storia dei ladri nel regno d'Italia* (Turin, 1869).

were formulated with the utmost respect that a representative of the government deserved and certainly a person, until otherwise proven, was innocent.

The package of papers was mailed and the speed of the royal post ensured that the reply arrived quickly. Sinibaldi signed four pages in accordance with protocol that were filled with rhetoric and positive sentiments. He concluded by stating "on his honor" that he was entirely estranged to that matter. Why not believe his word?[13]

No one wanted the truth to be known and the majority believed that it was not even necessary to make any great effort to seek it.

The only thing left were malicious questions. For example: how involved was the upright Bettino Ricasoli in this matter? He had the reputation of being an incorruptible man but on this occasion he exerted a great deal of effort dispersing the shares in the Southern Railways. Why did he accept to be its vice president? How was it possible that Gustavo Cavour, the brother of the "weaver" of our country's fabric, who had intervened on behalf of Bastogi, could have speculated on the company's shares? What role did Peruzzi, the man who praised the creation of a company entirely composed of Italians in Parliament, play in this matter? He obtained 10,000 shares and immediately ran to Paris to sell them.

The investigation committee had probably gathered a few more elements that could have been relevant to the case than what became publicly known. This information however never came to light because the files with this information no longer exist. All of the records, depositions, and the statements made by the committee members were stolen. The only thing that remained in the Chamber's archives was the cover of the file with the two corners of its first page slightly bent and the spine covered with some scribble marks along with two ink stains.

The theft was discovered in 1868, four years after the fact when Bastogi, who had resigned from the previous administration, was again elected into power by his citizens. A fellow representative believed this to

---

[13] V. Di Nardo, *Oh, mia Patria.*

be an insult to logic and common sense and began building a case to ensure that Bastogi did not return to power. It was in searching for documents that would legitimize the case for Bastogi's unsuitability for that role that they asked for that file that was archived in 1864. But the papers were missing…they had disappeared.

Giovanni Lanza, who in the meantime had been nominated as the President of the Chamber of Deputies, attempted to get to the bottom of this mystery by conducting a small administrative investigation. "I asked Representative A about the matter and he was not aware of anything. I interrogated Representative B and nothing came of this either. So I asked all of the other representatives and each of them, upon being called, merely shrugged their shoulders."[14]

It was immediately necessary to inform the magistrate. The King's attorney presented himself before the Chamber with his clerks to record the statements issued. "A few representatives were scandalized by seeing those who sought thieves carrying out their jobs in a hall of legislation and immediately filed lawsuits." President Lanza, to justify himself, was obliged to respond "by recounting every detail of what had happened and notified the nation regarding the theft of those papers from the archives. When this news was announced, all fell silent and this silence continues to this day."[15]

Bastogi, in a display of common sense that was greater than any of his supporters, resigned his seat in Parliament. He was voted into power again in 1868 and once again presented his letter of resignation. Victor Emanuel II, to compensate him, repaid him by naming him a count. A few years laer, Crispi nominated him as a senator.

In 1906, the railways became nationalized and the company founded by Bastogi, which owned the network and the structures, deposited a small fortune in its bank account that it applied (in part) towards the production of electricity. In 1963, as though it were right out of a script

---

[14] F. Boeri, *Storia dei ladri nel regno d'Italia* (Turin, 1869).
[15] Ibid.

that one has read numerous times over, the electric companies became nationalized as well and as usual Bastogi's company, which had yet again had its properties confiscated, deposited yet another frighteningly enormous sum of money in its bank account. This amount was enough to ensure that the Bastogi family entered in the elite class of bankers. Any time the newspapers mentioned him they did not omit that he represented all that was good in the Italian bourgeois. Michele Sindona and Roberto Calvi also carefully moved around amidst this bourgeois class.

CHAPTER 3

THE "INCAPABLE" DICTATOR SUPPORTER, THE "MOST CROOKED" CROOK, AND THE "MOST IGNORANT" IGNORAMUS

Ill-managed government, during those years following the Unification of Italy, seemed to be an infection that was capable of spreading at a frightening speed.

"Why must incredibly beautiful and wealthy Naples still need so many millions from these poor mountains?"[16] This rhetorical question posed by the *Gazzetta del Popolo* to its readers in reality served to denounce immoral finance practices. The news of these practices began to insistently leak out.

Cavour and the Piedmontese who launched the attack on the Kingdom of the Two Sicilies were convinced that Southern Italy was a territory with considerable economic potential. According to them, it was the poor management conducted by the Bourbon dynasty that ultimately had prevented a substantial development of the industrial sector in that area. Their optimistic predictions were a bit exaggerated, but there was some element of truth in their beliefs.

Shortly before the *Mille* soldiers made their entrance, the accountants had verified that the balance of the import/export trade of the Kingdom of Two Sicilies had included a profit of 35 million ducats. The shares in the Southern banks boasted share prices in the Paris stock exchange and thanks to their good reputation were used as currency in the rest of Europe. The money deposited in the Southern banks represented twice the amount of money in circulation in the rest of Italy.[17]

---

[16] *Gazzetta del Popolo*, March 22, 1861.
[17] R. Bracalini, *L'Italia prima dell'unità (1815-1860)* (Milan, 2001).

Therefore, the idea that the government of Turin should allot a few million lira to pay the salaries of the Southerners only a few months prior to their expected conquest rained upon the people like a cold shower.

What about Naples's gold?

The supporters of Garibaldi (first), then the dictatorial administration (next), and the new Kingdom of Italy (lastly) managed to squander a fortune. They dried up bank accounts, confiscated town halls and took what was in the safes, stole silverware, ceramics, and jewelry. The extraordinary aspect does not only lie in the frightening amount of money that was spent but also the speed with which even the last lira was consumed.[18]

This all began a few minutes after the first fleet arrived in the port of Marsala. Francesco Crispi presented himself before the mayor, proclaimed a State of Siege and called for the treasury's safes. He issued a receipt: the first autographed robbery in Sicily.[19]

Shortly after, the Red Shirts arrived in Palermo where their coffers were overflowing.

The Bank of Sicily, at the end of 1859, had turned to a group of architects because it grew necessary to reinforce the floors because the previous armored reinforcements were no longer sufficient to withstand the weight of the gold that was deposited. The only expense that no longer became necessary after the new government came into power was the previously mentioned one.

As soon as he arrived in the city he had just occupied, Giuseppe Garibaldi seized 2,178,818 lira of the 5 million that were deposited in the treasury. He left behind a piece of paper: "receipt for war expenses." It was understood that the newly formed State would have had to repay this loan and re-establish the order. That "autographed" document remained in the archives for several decades and in the accounting was calculated as a possession. When the administrators realized that nothing would ever be

---

[18] S. Jacini, *Due anni di politica italiana. Ricordi e impressioni* (Milan, 1868).
[19] L. Salera, *Garibaldi, Fauché e i Predatori del Regno del Sud. La vera storia dei piroscafi* Piemonte *e* Lombardo *nella spedizione dei Mille* (Naples, 2006).

returned to them, they relegated that document to their historical archives as evidence of a contribution made for the Unification of Italy.[20]

The other 3 million lira were withdrawn with the same degree of nonchalance and the same justifications were offered, though there are no documents attesting to who actually made the withdrawal and how much went to whom. Too many hands were involved in the management of the treasury's finances. Ippolito Nievo had an idea about what the expenses actually looked like but he wound up at the bottom of the sea along with all the documents that proved what he knew.

Between Catania and Messina, another twenty million lira were accumulated. However it was in Naples that the greatest amount of loot was retrieved. The banks held 33 million ducats, which were equivalent to approximately 165 million Piedmontese lira. This was three times the amount that Cavour requested on loan for the Second War of Independence in 1859. Colonel Fidel Kupa, a Hungarian who had voluntarily enrolled in Garibaldi's army sent a report to Cavour stating that the loot "amounted to around 90 million." Perhaps we should also add the 2 million gold coins that were the personal wealth of Francis II of Bourbon, who had carelessly left this amount in his bank account. At the exchange rate of the time that amount was equivalent to around 60 million lira. The management of this bank was assigned to Giuseppe Lambertini's "care" and he headed a committee that comprised both supporters of Mazzini and Garibaldi. In about a week or so, there was nothing left to manage because everything down to the last cent had been spent.[21]

The report issued by an officer of the Red Shirts was spiked with biting criticism. He reported "a total state of disorder with a total lack of discipline" that only served to invoke "unmanageable confusion." The daily expenses incurred went beyond all imagination.

"In such a manner," concluded Kupa, "the coffers quickly remained empty." Since there were suppliers that required payment: "we required

---

[20] Archivio storico, Banco di Sicilia.
[21] R. Martucci, *L'invenzione dell'Italia unita. 1855-1864* (Milan, 1999).

money and were forced to state that there was none to be had. Garibaldi ordered that we should inform the bankers that it was their duty to provide these funds by threatening them at rifle point. The first of the bankers from Naples arrived and handed us one or two million lira."[22] These were small amounts compared to the patriots' enormous requirements that needed to be met. They managed to quickly spend all of those funds as well and required further intervention from Turin.

That small treasure, in the right proportion, was stolen and wasted in order to maintain the military contingency, however, no one was exactly certain how large or consistent this contingency actually was.

A voluntary army is, by definition, one that pays less attention to the hierarchical rules, which any other regular army is particularly careful to obey. The Red Shirts pushed their limits and behaved themselves in a "Garibaldi" style. They were "volunteers" in the sense that each one voluntarily did what they felt like doing. They often left one division to join another. They took breaks and then they came back. They made themselves available to carry out certain tasks but then decided it was more convenient to carry out another.

What was the result? "No company knows the exact number or names of the soldiers that comprise their ranks." These were the words of Fidel Kupa, who was an eyewitness to the entire affair.

"These soldiers pass from one company to the next so that the size of the company may grow or diminish. The soldiers that have received their pay, once they have spent five days here, then pass to another company and there they receive another paycheck. A contingent of 10,000 men may wind up costing as much as one numbering 30,000."[23]

Slightly more than 25,000 men distributed 60,000 coats that, in half a day, ended up sold on the black market at a low price. Even in Florence in the "military's clothing warehouse there were 700 articles of clothing

---

[22] C. Benso Conte Di Cavour, *Carteggio. La liberazione del Mezzogiorno* (Bologna, 1961). Colonel Kupa's report is dated October 18, 1860.
[23] Ibid. Colonell Kupa's report is dated October 18, 1860.

missing, worth about 30,000 *scudi*."[24] Upon retrieving an order placed for horses, 200 were lost in transit.[25]

There were departments that had their entire rank of officers filled, including the regiment's band but that could not count one soldier. This is even better than the *ragazzi della Via Pal* where, amongst the many decorated officers, only poor Nemecek had no stripes to his uniform: but at least they could count at least one soldier.

It was rare that there were any "incidents" during the distribution of the soldiers' salaries. Ippolito Nievo, in Sicily, took part in an argument with a commander that was looking to receive a hundred more salaries than he effectively needed.[26]

In Naples, even the sub-commissioner of war was assigned to dispense the salaries to the soldiers and officials. He asked Captain Rossi, who was responsible for handling the *Ai Quattro venti* company, the list of names. There were 188 soldiers and 135 officers. The sub-commissioner immediately verified himself that the troop was composed of 111 men (those who were absent had already transferred to Milazzo) and 58 officials. Captain Rossi withheld the pay of 70 soldiers and 77 officers.[27]

Every once in a while a piece of evidence emerges that exposes some fraudulent activity. For example, when the Minister of War ordered that "payment be issued to Major Niederhausen" who was leaving "with his battalion in organization": "in organization" meant that the battalion did not actually exist. The battalion was a virtual one. General Acerbi attempted to offer a reasonable objection: with the coffers of the treasury empty it would not be possible to offer salaries in advance to military com-

---

[24] *Eco delle Romagne*, February 12, 1861.

[25] R. Martucci, *L'invenzione dell'Italia unita 1855-1864* (Milan, 1999).

[26] Cavour, *Carteggio*. The episode is described in detail in the chapter on Ippolito Nievo.

[27] Ibid. Letter of the deputy commissioner of war, Giuseppe Guccione, to the general mayor, dated, Palermo, August 23, 1860.

panies that did not yet exist.... But there was nothing to be done. He was told that he had to issue payment.[28]

The confusion was fueled by the structure of command itself, which, in theory, was divided into three parts: the Ministry of War, the general staff, and the inspectorate. In times of war, with any army at one's disposal, it is already difficult enough to divide the decision-making by three. In this case, each one made decisions without consulting the other two entities with the result that these orders were redundant or often contradicted one another. To speak of "each" of these three entities is actually an arbitrary simplification because each one was further divided into chiefs, vice-chiefs, secretaries and commissioners that each had their own duties and prerogatives that they needed to defend. Sometimes they needed to defend their decisions merely to affirm their authority.

The only orders that effectively stood a chance of being carried out were those personally issued by Garibaldi himself. Often, however, he changed his mind with the result being that he issued two conflicting orders regarding the same matter, effectively negating himself. This was the case when he decided to establish a cavalry and the he decided that it was no longer necessary. This resulted in the nomination of the officers (and the costs that such officers incurred) with no service.[29]

A Piedmontese or Bourbon division could count anywhere between 8 and 10,000 soldiers. Garibaldi's divisions numbered approximately 2,500-3000. The number of officers, on the other hand, remained the same, which means that the Red Shirts employed 5 times as many ranked officials than necessary. For every twenty soldiers, one was a ranked officer as opposed to one out of every four soldiers. Sometimes, some soldiers even promoted themselves. "He pretended to be an officer and proceeded to give orders," Nicola Fabrizi, the Minister under the dictatorship supporter Mordini, complained in a written letter. "Countless officers, either

---

[28] Ibid. Letter of the general mayor, Giuseppe Acerbi, to the secretary of defense, dated, Palermo, July 17, 1860.
[29] R. Martucci, *L'invenzione dell'Italia unita. 1855-1864* (Milan, 1999).

without a license or that have been discharged, continue to wear their uniforms and cause trouble."[30]

Money was squandered, but was additionally stolen through well organized, scientifically orchestrated schemes.

According to Colonel Kupa, who confided in his Hungarian friend Stefano Turr, "large sums of money were subtracted by Agostino Bertani, but not for personal use. They were used for the Republican cause...."[31] In a matter of a few years, many newspaper companies were purchased and established. It is not difficult to imagine what funds were used.

Did this theft limit itself to the coffers of political parties? This is improbable. Francesco Giglianetti, the Secretary General for the Ministry of Internal Affairs wrote that he had come to know "from a reliable source that many Red Shirts, who had left to fight the war in a miserable state, had returned with their pockets filled with 1000 lira banknotes."[32]

Cavour was informed that Giambattista Fauché, general director of the Rubatino shipping company (the one responsible for transporting the *Mille* soldiers) had granted "commissions everywhere to acquire ships, materials, and provisions without any particular need. These were just acquired out of the desire to spend. He ordered from Genoa two thousand marine uniforms."[33] He ordered these uniforms for a military contingent that did not yet exist.

This was a provisory government that was comprised of troublemakers.

They imagined that they would "reimburse" those that had suffered wrongdoings at the hands of the Bourbon monarchs. As predicted, throngs of people showed up claiming to be children, brothers, and fathers of

---

[30] Cavour, *Carteggio*. Circular letter of the secretary of defense to the general mayor of the southern army, dated, Palermo, October 6, 1860.

[31] Cavour, *Carteggio*. Colonel Kupa's report is dated October 18, 1860.

[32] Ibid. Letter of Francesco Guglianetti to Luigi Carlo Farini, dated October 7, 1860.

[33] Ibid. Letter of Francesco Guglianetti to Luigi Carlo Farini, dated October 7, 1860.

victims. They presented themselves before the appropriate offices to claim what was theirs by right. Numerous liberal patriots complained that they had been tortured in the past and present. The daughter of Pisacane obtained a pension of 60 ducats and the sisters of Agesilao Milano received 2,000 ducats for his death sentence pronounced for his having made an attempt on the life of the king. Checks were issued for 10... 15... 18,000 lira to people that were considered "highly inept or infamous."[34]

Those who found themselves in positions of power began to think of themselves. Antonio Scialoja wrote himself a voucher for 200,000 francs. The signature was the same for the person both issuing and receiving the check. He figured it would be worthwhile to write another check for his father: another 200,000 francs, with signatures that at least seemed slightly different. Raffaele Conforti, who had been a minister in 1848 for a few months, wrote himself a check for 60,000 ducats. This is more or less the amount that he would have received had he remained in office from 1848 to 1861. Aurelio Saliceti, a magistrate, made due with a pension of 2,250 ducats.

Expenses, profits, and gifts. Alexandre Dumas, a supporter of Garibaldi, handed the Piedmontese government a list of reimbursements that amounted to 83, 690 lira which was paid in cash. It was so easy to request money that he immediately made another request for 7,743 and was paid without any problems. At that point, he decided to write a book, without specifying its themes, and received an advance of 4,000 lira.

So why feel guilty about anything? "In Naples, a sergeant that accompanied Lieutenant Santi, upon returning from the Bank of Naples with 20,000 gold francs ran off with the entire sum while the lieutenant was in the restroom."[35] In those same days, 20,000 lira went missing from the office for the administration of lots and 5,000 lira went missing from the office of records and stamps.[36]

---

[34] R. Martucci, *L'invenzione dell'Italia unita. 1855-1864* (Milan, 1999).
[35] *Giornale di Napoli*, October 6, 1861.
[36] *Lampo degli Italiani*, January 11, 1861.

A patriotic robbery also took place in Genoa. On the 6th of May, 1862, a gang broke into the Bartolomeo Parodi and Son's Bank at 2 in the afternoon. They were aggressive and resolute; they bound two of the employees and made off with 800,000 lira: an important sum of money for that time.[37] The owner of the bank announced in several newspapers that he would have awarded a sum of 60,000 lira for anyone who helped to catch the criminals. The promise of that money worked.

On the 8th of May, the trawler *Amor di Patria* was leaving its port heading towards the Black Sea. It was loaded with gold nuggets. Perhaps because it was spied, shortly afterward the steamer *Montebello*, with 12 *carabinieri* on board blocked its passage and the loot emerged from the subsequent investigation. Aside from the money, there were also a few guns, 4 rifles and 2 Orsini bombs found. How could one deny such evidence? They eventually confessed but they wanted to specify that the robbery was done with the sole purpose of financing other expeditions, such as that of the *Mille*, to seize both Venice and Rome. On the 5th of May, a celebration was held to honor those of Garibaldi's soldiers had departed from Quarto. Many authorities had arrived to participate in the celebrations. Amongst those officials was a colonel who "proposed to stage a robbery and split the loot." Half would have gone to the actual thieves and the rest would have gone to fund the revolutions in Venice and Rome. One of the thieves, Pietro Ceneri, showed the passport that the official had forgotten upon his departure from Genoa.[38]

It was impossible to limit the wild fury of such villains. Admiral Di Negro, who attempted to enforce some of the smaller rules and regulations so that theft could not occur so blatantly, was forced to leave his post as commander of the arsenal in Naples. "There, the average crook was so well-organized that from one day to the next weapons, clothing, and ammunition would disappear: in other words, everything. Di Negro, hav-

---

[37] F. Boeri, *Storia dei ladri nel regno d'Italia* (Turin, 1869).
[38] Ibid.

ing attempted to pose some obstacles to this thievery put his life at risk. Now he is obliged to travel accompanied escorted by the *carabinieri*."[39]

The national guard present in Carbonara had to be dissolved because "several soldiers had joined the cause of the brigands," and had subsequently opened fire upon a military squad "that had been left in charge of guarding certain military effects."[40] The civic guards of Castecicala, "a village near the town of Nola," were also abolished by lieutenant's decree. "Within that town there was a faction of individuals with family ties to the group of brigands that infested the outskirts."[41]

After all, the *camorra* was actually set loose by Garibaldi himself. He entered Naples escorted by criminals who had been converted to patriots. They had the faces of thugs but wore the hat with the tricolor feather. Armed with their knives at their waists they guarded the General's wagon down the streets of the city. The criminals actually remained even after Garibaldi left. They actually received some benefits. Marianna De Crescenzo, the sister of one of the *camorra* bosses, received 12 ducats per month. All of the most prominent women of the *camorra* received something. The *camorra*, as an organization, found itself managing 75,000 ducats "to distribute to the poorest members." They were also useful to compensate a great many lower ranking hoodlums that from that moment onward were even more grateful and loyal to the bosses of Neapolitan crime.

How can one be amazed if whatever the *camorra* said was as good as law? This is even truer because the person who was supposed to put a stop to this criminal organization was Giorgio Pallavicini Trivulzio, a dictatorship supporter and a man whom Cavour considered "highly incapable."[42] He even had a few skeletons in his closet. He presented himself as a "martyr of the *Spielberg*" and it was a half-truth. It was his behavior

---

[39] *Il Giornale Ufficiale*, May 8, 1861.
[40] *Il Giornale Ufficiale*, May 4, 1861.
[41] *Il Giornale Ufficiale*, May 16, 1861.
[42] Cavour, *Carteggio*. Letter of Cavour to Luigi Carlo Farini, dated, Turin, November 1, 1860.

that brought about the arrest of Silvio Pellico and Federico Confalonieri and while he was incarcerated, his behavior was hardly exemplary.

In Naples, his desire to do anything was nil. He showed up at parties and official events, so that he could dignify the event with his presence, shook some hands, exchanged a few words, and then returned to the building that was his assigned residence. He took it upon himself to do absolutely nothing.

The administration was in a state of ruin. When Filippo Curletti, Cavour's personal spy, landed in Naples, he found the city "in the midst of the most incredible chaos." He commented, "The army was full of women: Milady White and Admiral Emilia were the heroines. The nights turned into orgies. Garibaldi was no longer recognizable: when he was not busy satisfying his desire for popularity, reaping praise in the streets, he passed his time with Milady and Alexandre Dumas who were always by his side. He saw nothing and did nothing. He merely left things flow whichever way the current took them."[43]

Carlo Alianello, in his work *L'eredità della Priora*, managed to depict a capable individual and in a few lines was able to summarize a complex sociological analysis. "First Garibladi was the type of person that took nothing for himself, but he kept friends in his company that 'ate' a great deal and he enjoyed first lavishing them with compliments, then presents, then something, then something else.... Then he had to return to Turin for a loan. From noblemen that we once were, we have become beggars. Farini said that he wanted to die a poor man... but how would that be possible? He takes in a salary of 11,000 ducats a month!"

The people who were supposed to be protected where locked in their homes because the streets were roamed by drunkards and criminals. It became difficult even to shop for anything because the prices of provisions had skyrocketed. One was even obliged to pay for water.

---

[43] E. Bianchini Braglia, ed, *La verità sugli uomini e sulle cose del regno d'Italia* (Modena, 2005).

Carlo Alianello continued: "They have even stolen the wool from our mattresses... everything... down to the last coin.... How much did they steal? A preposterous amount!"

The state of disorder prompted Garibaldi to nominate a certain Giordano as the head of a given group of officials. "He represented the tyrannical past and the people proceeded to kill him." "Three Bourbon monarchy supporters" who frequented the offices of the Secretary for Internal Affairs "were kicked out of the building." But "the former director of Internal Affairs, Celesti, a man who was hated in the past, and who all believed had fled, reappeared at the side of the current director with bodyguards that defended him from insults."

"A young man from Mancilepre" found himself as the new governor of Palermo. The one from Aci "was refused by the people who did not want him." A certain Pancaldi, who was supposed to take charge of Messina, "will probably be received with rifle shots."[44]

Crispi "demonstrated his miserable ineptitude." Monsignor Ugdulena and the Baron Pisani "were certainly gentlemen, but were also clearly inept." They "put their finances in the hands of that incredibly crooked and ignorant man, B."[45]

The Bourbon administration, which was built upon a network of efficient offices and was modeled after the French system of prefectures, had completely disintegrated. In place of the former governors, which had been either been forced to flee or simply removed from their offices, dozens of new ones appeared. Similar to the 2,000 small and large towns, National Guard posts were improvised. These were placed in the care of notable figures with presumed liberal tendencies that were often merely seeking jobs. They had been considered excess baggage for many years, were infinitely insistent, and had received standard "patriotic" accolades.

---

[44] Cavour, *Carteggio.* La Farina's letter, dated June 18, 1860.
[45] Cavour, *Carteggio.* La Farina's letter, dated July 2, 1860.

Giuseppe Massari wrote to Cavour: "For 15 intendency jobs, we already have 750 applications."[46]

---

[46] Cavour, *Carteggio*. Giuseppe Massari's letter to Count Cavour, dated October 21, 1860.

CHAPTER 4

THIEVES IN PARLIAMENT

In order to face the skyrocketing expenses, the only thing left to do was to raise taxes. The newspapers of 1866 reported that 22 million Italians were facing taxes that were even higher than 19 million of their neighboring Prussians. Guglielmo Rustow explained why: "The Italian system of government does not employ people to meet the needs of the people, but to create jobs for their friends: in this manner there will never be enough money.[47]

Effectively if the expenses continued to grow at this rate, even what was collected would never be sufficient.

Everyone learned how to steal and with the excuse of the Unification of Italy, everyone preoccupied themselves with handling their own best interests.

It should be understood that the people stealing were not merely those who were stealing in order to put food on their tables: this could at least have been somewhat justifiable. The majority of those stealing from the public treasury were those who were in important offices seeking further affirmations. I will venture to say that the higher the rank of the thief, the more the theft appeared shameless. It was as though their rank implied that they could behave with arrogant nonchalance.

The school of "fraud" boasted many professors that went on to teach many students that were already naturally gifted. There were no obstacles and there was no remorse.

---

[47] W. Rustow, *La guerra italiana del 1860 descritta politicamente e militarmente* (Milan, 1862).

An example? The matter regarding the transfer of the capital from Turin to Florence to cater to Napoleon III's desires and allow all to believe that Italy had given up on conquering Rome: at least for a little while. In reality, it was all a clever ruse and the first to distrust the protocol agreement were the ones who actually wrote it. Sometimes, it is necessary to perform such actions for show.

Therefore, the meeting halls for the representatives and senators had to be prepared. They chose to readapt the hall of "the *Cinquecento*." The Minister of Public Works, Stefano Jacini, assigned the task to the architect Carlo Falcolnieri, who was considered a luminary in his field. He held many titles and had completed many important works: enough to fill two pages. His work included the Office of the Minister of Public Works all the way to the Inspectorate of Civil Engineering.

The project for its renovation was enormous, not so much because it would take a long time but because of its huge expense. Could one really spare any expense in designing the seat of legislative power of the new kingdom? The renovation projects obtained the general approval of the experts and the members of Parliament. Falconieri also signed a pamphlet that explained the architectural philosophy that had inspired him and actually risked to cause a small diplomatic incident when he stated that his work was "motivated by the supposition" that Florence would only be a stepping stone towards Rome.

"It is with this thought in mind, as he was working, that he made another supposition. Supposing that Menabrea was able to heroically and patriotically steal Rome from the Pope: he, Falconieri, could have stolen something from the Kingdom of Italy. He shared his 'supposition' with his three friends: Fontana, Gori, Bartolini" who were his closest collaborators. "The three men found the supposition to be very logical, useful, and patriotic."[48]

They stole by inflating their provisions and they skimmed a bit off the top. They inflated orders and expected bribes on any acquisitions

---

[48] F. Boeri, *Storia dei ladri nel regno d'Italia* (Turin, 1869).

made. They exaggerated. They presented bills and notes where there were numerous teams of workers that actually only existed on paper. The only thing that was real was the salary that the architects received. Since they needed to provide both first and last names for their employees, they gave the names of the clergy responsible for the *Duomo* of Florence. They also mentioned the bishop's vicar.

How could they not be discovered? They were arrested, tried, and condemned.[49] Falconieri received a sentence of 3 and one-half years, while Fontana and Gori received one of 3 years. Bartolini was condemned to 7 months. Justice was not even heavy-handed with them, particularly because they only carried out one quarter of their sentence. After 14 months, Falconieri was set free and began to work once again.

Another example? Four or five men, while living in Turin, devised a complex plan to take possession of a noble man's property. He was very wealthy, very sick, and very naïve.

The victim was the Marquis of Fuente di Villa Hermosa, Giuseppe d'Aboanza, who was of Spanish descent. He held the noble title of "don" and was a resident of Genoa, though he often traveled to Turin where he rented an elegant apartment in the Svizzera Hotel. He suffered from gangrene and had periodic flare ups. In Piedmont, he had an episode of pain and high fever and anyone who encountered him believed that his time on this earth was over.

How did this information become public knowledge? A group of swindlers approached him on his deathbed and convinced him to sign a will that the notary Martina registered. According to the official document, the Marquis Fuente authorized a salary of 150 lira per month to Giambattista Mannelli, who had initially been a Franciscan monk but that then decided to abandon his robe (it is not difficult to imagine why) and once again became a layman. Another salary was to be dispensed to the wife of the surveyor Filippo Berdoati, with yearly concession of 2,000 lira. Felice Casilli, a clerk for the Ministry of grace and Justive, was slated

---

[49] The sentence was pronounced on August 21, 1867.

to receive a salary of 1,500 lira per year. But the biggest paycheck was destined for Giovanni Vignali, a Neapolitan living in Piedmont. He had all of his papers in order and was considered a liberal patriot.

It goes without saying that the dying man did not know any of the people whom he was so generously assisting. The notary drafted the document and only at the last minute called forth all of the witnesses in Don Giuseppe d'Aboanza's bedroom to confirm his last will and testament. These witnesses, however, could not hear any phrases that made any sense. He spoke in fragments and was probably in a delirious state: "ten... obsequious... throne...." Who knows what the man was thinking as he lay there dying,

The true heirs of the dying man threw a fit and managed to prove that they were victims of fraud.

The "brains" of the operation was Vignali, who boasted a truly frightening resumè.[50] He had been the head of the Superior Council of Education, a position that had been assigned to him by the Minister Mancini. Then he took on the role of Prime Minister but resigned after only a few months. From the records detailing this meeting, this statement emerged: "Minister Petruzzi has written to me insisting that I stay and at the very least requests that I declare that the resignation was of my own volition." He remained in his position, but it resulted as though he had taken a leave of absence. The police investigations confirmed this fraudulent act. In a matter of a few months, the courts sentenced the men in question. The Court of Appeals confirmed the sentence immediately afterwards.[51]

The sentence was as follows: Mannelli and Vignali both received 7 years of prison, whule Berdoati and Casilli received a six year sentence. Casilli, however, never served a day of his prison sentence because from his privileged job as a clerk, he had discovered his sentence in advance and managed to flee abroad before he was arrested.

---

[50] *Gazzetta del Popolo*, February 18, 1866. In reference to the news of the hearing in the Corte d'assise on February 15.

[51] The sentence was pronounced on March 10, 1866.

The notary was not convicted of any crime because, according to the magistrates, he had only done his job. From the beginning of the foundation of Italy, notaries can certify the most ridiculous things yet they are not responsible for any of their actions.

There were thieves of all types that were armed with the wildest imaginations. Rather than govern Italy, however, they chose to tear it to pieces.

CHAPTER 5

"THE NEIGHBORHOOD WISE GUYS" IN THE NINETEENTH-CENTURY BANKS

The carelessness of the political class during the Unification of Italy has been well documented in the episodes surrounding the scandal that erupted surrounding the Bank of Rome.

Who were the protagonists? The neighborhood wise guys of the nineteenth century.

They showed the unscrupulousness of busboys, the wastefulness of institutional committees and the complacency of royalty. What they designed was a systematic organization capable of plundering the State's resources in such a way that they could transform public utilities into private profits.

The key to properly understanding the attitude of that generation of speculators lies in a meeting organized in Rome in September of 1870.

In the days immediately following the fall of *Porta Pia* in Rome while the rest of Italy was celebrating the conquest of the capital, a meeting was called in Palazzo Sciarra. This meeting has been often ignored in the annals of Italy's history, though it is a benchmark in establishing the DNA that the managerial class of the Risorgimento possessed (and therefore their children and their children's children).

Many Roman aristocrats were present at the meeting including several cardinals and bankers including (could he really have missed this meeting?) Pietro Bastogi (the same one from the railway deal). Also present were several bankers from the North including Pietro Brambilla, Giovanni Bombrini, Antonio Allevi, and Giacinto Balbis. According to the reconstruction of events furnished by Filippo Mazzonis, the participants organized themselves in such a way as to ensure the participation of each member in a coordinated fashion.[52] In this context, they devised a plan for a newly conquered Rome that would not become an industrial city. In a certain sense, the upper echelon of the Italian capitalists did not want large groups of workers that coalesced in factories and could ignite into a labor union protest in a brief time. But mostly, they were not interested in an economic prospect that required any medium-term effort with the risks that any business might have. Who on earth would make them settle for that? The objective of these opportunists was not to work, invest, or contribute to the future of this country, without even considering that this could actually be very profitable in the long run. Their objective was to get rich quick.

Therefore, they decided to place their bets on safe investments so that the money they used would rapidly return to their wallets with interest. In this manner of thinking, the most logical investment to make was in the construction business. Rome was once again to be the capital of a nation that would have soon come to know a great demand for residences. There was much money to be made, and effortlessly.

The landowners would have started with selling their land at very high prices. The buildings built on those lands would have become immediately available with considerable advantages for businesses. It would be even better if they didn't have to put up the starting capital but rather from a loan issued by a third party.

Herein lies the premise behind the scandal of the Bank of Rome.

Then one must also consider the approximation with which the credit system's foundation was built. In fact, it was abandoned to the whims of single bankers who were caught up in trying to deal with a market that grew disproportionately over the course of a decade. They operated with the presumptuousness of a parvenu.

A centralized institution where the financial policies of the country could be established did not exist. There were six credit institutions that

---

[52] F. Mazzonis, *Roma conquistata*, in *Convegno di storia della Chiesa*, La Mendola August 31-September 5, 1971.

were authorized to mint coins. This was actually an anomaly that had been inherited from the time prior to the Unification when each kingdom had autonomous exchange offices. It would have been opportune for the government to intervene and unify all of these entities immediately but the decision to do so kept getting delayed. To be honest, the Ministries that were authorized to handle the matter did very little to regulate the activities of these mini-banks, with the result being that financial situation was in a state of complete disarray. When rules are not codified it is easy to take advantage of them.

The imminent and most evident danger was that there was very little discipline displayed by the banks. In June of 1884, the periodical *Forche Caudine,* published a very vitriolic comment on this situation. "Our banking system is still feudal. The only Institution that is capable of exerting any authority is the Bank of Rome, but it is represented by an oligarchy, a privileged class: the merchants. They are not industrials or businessmen. They are speculators that victimize those to whom they choose to loan money at exorbitant interest rates but who receive conditions that are extremely favorable."

This diagnosis, a brave one, came from the pen of Pietro Sbarbaro, a journalist with solid knowledge of the economy. He was capable of combining a rare scientific ability with morals that prevented him from accepting blatant wrongdoings. It is for this reason that he was never offered any prestigious positions and did not have access to the aristocratic salons of the capital.

"It is to this oligarchy," he added, "that the Bank of Rome, presided by Tanlongo, concedes its favors. There are also favors offered to the families of politicians who always manage to obtain a bill of exchange with no real term. It remains closed in their wallets and is constantly extended and renewed until some day, thanks to a favor obtained, even that piece of paper becomes worthless." He was incisive in his prose and ruthless in his content.

The Tanlongo that the article mentions was Bernardo Tanlongo. He was an intriguing man who came from a modest family yet had a very finely tuned mind. He barely knew how to read and write but was incredibly versatile when it came to arithmetic. If the numbers in question happened to correspond to money, however, he became unbeatable. Furthermore, he possessed a natural ability to attract the attention of powerful men and to keep their friendship.

At the time of the Republic in Rome under Giuseppe Mazzini, he was a spy for the French.[53] Cavour, many years later, bestowed upon him the task of offering consistent sums of money to several cardinals in order to "soften" the Vatican's stance regarding the Unification of Italy. He was a man for all seasons. He was the man most trusted by the Jesuits and the *Propaganda Fide* but this did not stop him from meeting the wishes of the Grand Master Mason along with all of the "brothers" to whom he was introduced.

It goes without saying that he was always welcome at the royal court.

The "gentleman" king had a large amount of debts and he considered it a blessing from God when people could loan him something. Umberto I, who was his successor to the throne, was not particularly fond of Tanlongo, but he was still welcome at the royal court due to the fact that he was in good graces with the king's wife and the king's two lovers: the Countess Santafiora and, most importantly the Duchess Litta.

We still have a letter written by Queen Margherita dated December 7, 1887 in which she coquettishly complains that he stops by the palace too rarely. "Are you holding a grudge?" the monarch asked from her throne. "You almost compel me to ask you to come on purpose. Dear Mr. Tanlongo, can you not imagine how much more your witty banter amuses me than that of the most humorous speakers in my court?" An invitation to dinner ensued, and to tickle the palate, she also included a brief description of the menu. "The sweetest addition to my pastry desserts would be if you would be pleased to arrive at 8 for dinner in my company."

---

[53] P. Tanlongo, *Una parte della corrispondenza di Bernardo Tanlongo* (Rome, 1893).

The first effects of the scandal were felt in 1889. Until the market continued to expand, it corrected itself. When, however, that growth began to stall, the credit, which had been inflated like a balloon began to show its fragility.

The credit institutions had disproportionately increased the amount of paper money in circulation, without the corresponding amount of gold. They suddenly found themselves exposed with their clients. The investors became quite alarmed.

The Bank of Rome felt the worst blow, because it was the bank, in the realm of general irresponsibility, that had exaggerated more than the other banks. With the utmost nonchalance, it had allowed for the printing of millions of banknotes without considering the principles of economics and ignoring all logic and common sense.

Bernardo Tanlongo, up until that point and through friendship and generous "gifts," had managed to silence the rumors and avoid the scandal breaking out. But there came a time when it was no longer possible for him to contain it. The government was forced to nominate an investigation committee to check the accounts and balances and immediately placed Senator Giacomo Alvisi in charge of coordinating the effort. Shortly thereafter, he discovered a deficit of 9 million lira, which for the time was a monstrous sum of money. This was nothing compared to the true proportions of the debt.

On June 30, 1891, the Parliament addressed this problem for the first time: the Prime Minister, Antonio Starabba di Rudinì; the Minister of Finance, Luigi Luzzati; the President of the Assembly, Domenico Farina. In a fully-attended meeting, it became common knowledge that the bank had printed 128 million lira worth of banknotes but that their reserves only covered 58 million lira.

Just this piece of disconcerting news was enough to frighten the representatives who could only imagine the backlash that would ensue on the market. They pretended not to know anything and chose to know nothing further, with a completely hypocritical justification. "An investigation of this sort is useful for the government but it is not useful to render this information public."

Senator Alvisi, who had already prepared a detailed report, did not understand but adapted to the request. He gathered all of his papers in a chest and resumed his work as an accountant for the bank. He was found dead before the government retained it necessary to ask for more detailed information regarding his work. That man must have been one of the few who took his government-appointed job seriously. In contrast to the vast number of his colleagues, he did not bother trying to cover up his documents or modify the declarations made therein. He did not try to hide the obvious or falsify the papers.

He must have realized that his efforts did not matter to the Parliament and the rest of the government. They were more interested in letting things go than in discovering flaws. Perhaps it was to prevent his efforts from being "misplaced," he sent a copy of his work to the economist Leone Wollemborg who showed it to another prestigious economist, Maffeo Pantaleoni. Pantaleoni decided that silence would equal infamy and he contacted two members of Parliament of two opposing factions: the Republican of the extreme Left, Napoleon Colajanni and the ecclesiastical moralist of the Right, Lodovico Gavazzi. The issue was once again brought to the attention of the politicians.

In the meantime, the government was in the hands of Giovanni Giolitti, who entertained the notion of ridding himself of the problem by talking a good game and then fumbling when it came time to actually dealing with the problem. In front of the government, his declarations were accented by very severe tones. "If there is corruption, the hand of justice will deliver a blow to all involved." This statement was followed by: "The government has decided that it will get to the bottom of this matter." However, he then proceeded to personally hide six binders of compromising papers.[54]

---

[54] Archivio storico della Camera dei deputati, minutes of the parliamentary meetings, 1891.

Why did he bother? Giolitti was only marginally involved in the matters at hand. He was accused of having taken advantage of the bank by requesting a loan for 60,000 lira that the Commander Cantoni delivered to Giolitti's secretary. But this liberal representative could justify this loan without too much trouble. That sum was requested and officially used by the government. A highly detailed eight-page report stated that due to the expenses incurred by the Ministry of Internal Affairs in dealing with the Sicilian *Fasci*, the coffers were empty. At the same time, in Genoa, the celebrations honoring Christopher Columbus were to take place but they were in jeopardy due to lack of funds. It is for this reason that it was decided to "request an advance that would have been repaid with interest." He was capable of demonstrating that, several days prior, 61,500 lira had been returned.[55] They attempted to tarnish his name again by accusing him of having obtained 40 or 50,000 lira. Pietro, the eldest son of Tanlongo, was the person who actually gave him this money. Giolitti, however, denied it. There was no evidence and those directly affected, starting from the "mailman" did not confirm anything.

Those who found themselves in more serious trouble were his political adversaries whose speeches oozed moralism. The heroes of the Risorgimento had not restricted themselves from seizing some public funds. The first 69,000 lira went to the Representative Francesco Pais Serra, a nobleman from Sardinia who was sympathetic to Garibaldi's cause. Another 60,000 lira went to the Minister of Education Ferdinando Martini. Others who received money included: the representative from L'Aquila Federico Colajanni (a friend of Depretis), the lawyer from Siracusa Emilio Bufardeci (a friend of Francesco Crispi) and the Hon. Alessandro Narducci, a friend of both.

These "legendary" historical figures' names were tarnished. Both Edoardo Arbib and Raffaello Giovagnoli, received bribes as well. They were two of the *Mille* soldiers.

---

[55] G. Natale, *Giolitti e gli italiani* (Milan, 1949).

The list of clients who were in debt included the Baron Gennaro Sambiase Sanseverino of San Donato, though it is not certain with how much diligence he carried out his job as the president of the Parliamentary Commission for Banking Reform. Ranieri Simonelli the formere Secretary General for the Ministry of Agriculture, and member of the aforementioned commission also had not repaid his loan.

Money was also given to the journalist Claudio Pancrazi, to the director of the *Il Tempo* newspaper in Venice, Roberto Galli, and to Giovanni Nicotera who needed 15,000 lira for his newspaper *La Tribuna*.[56]

The director of the *Gazzetta Piemontese* of Turin, Luigi Roux, wanted to earn money in a more appropriate manner. Since he had a newspaper at his disposal and since he had been elected representative, he managed to be assigned as the head of the Press for the Ministry of Internal Affairs. Are there any objections?

It seemed as though the Parliament was composed of paupers who were forced into debt to carry onward. The list of those who benefitted, in alphabetical order, began with Baldassare Avanzini and ended with Seabstiano Tecchio. Ulisse Papa and the fiery Marziale Capo were also on the list.

The former Prime Minister, Benedetto Cairoli passed away. His wife recognized the debts he owed and chose to sell their villa in Belgirate. The debts were justified with the costs incurred for the man's medical care and the members of government stated that the king had offered to personally pay the man's debts himself. It is not difficult to imagine that these were all explanations that were constructed so as not to cause serious damage to the noble family's wealth, though they were already in serious trouble.

It was therefore not out of personal interest that Giovanni Giolitti attempted to skew the details surrounding the scandal. He probably believed that by uncovering the reasons behind it would have provoked a

---

[56] E. Magrì, *I ladri di Roma. Scandalo della Banca Romana: politici, giornalisti eroi del Risorgimento all'assalto del denaro pubblico* (Milan, 1993).

dangerous backlash on institutions of the newly formed national government. He had to take into consideration that it was better to pardon a few scoundrels than to risk the loss of favorability in the public opinion.

He grossly miscalculated.

CHAPTER 6

CRISPI, PRIME MINISTER: CUCKOLDED BY HIS BUTLER

Tanlongo, the banker, along with another colleague, Cesare Lazzaroni, was arrested on January 18, 1893. The following week, on January 23, the Prime Minister was obliged to answer a series of questions. He revealed that the circulation of clandestine funds amounted to 63,784,792 lira. The credit system was about to burst.[57]

Seven "sages" were selected amongst the members of Parliament and after 8 months of research, they presented the fruit of their labor: a 200-page report. The technicians who examined the text concluded that it was "excellent."

The text described in great detail all of the credit mechanisms employed that resulted in the current deficit. This was all precious advice to those bankers who would have to follow stringent rules and regulations. But the "sages" were reticent when it came down to dealing with attributing any responsibilities. When faced with addressing the problem, they all answered with elegant verbal acrobatics and therefore, ultimately, did not answer anything. The only criticism that they offered that was both energetic and without exception, was reserved for Giolitti. They revealed that he had hindered investigation efforts, going to extremes to ensure that documents considered invaluable went missing.

Due to some indiscretions on some corrupt politicians, it became necessary to wait for Tanlongo's trial, which occurred in spring of 1894. The accused, the first concession offered by the magistrate, was not accused of bankruptcy fraud, as he should have, but for a series of marginal crimes.

---

[57] Archivio storico della Camera dei deputati, minutes of parliamentary meetings, 1893.

He was accused of having conceded personal bank loans and of having exceeded in emitting banknotes.

The defense reacted by stating that those irregularities were solicited by the government itself and had interceded directly to secure loans for certain politicians and to finance governmental news bulletins.

Which men and which newspapers were being called into question? The names and last names in addition to all the surrounding circumstances were in those papers that had been lost.

Therefore, the trial, this was the second concession offered by the magistrate, resulted in the banker's absolution. This however prompted harsh comments from many members of Parliament who did not hesitate to criticize Giolitti. They believed his behavior in the entire matter was wrong and that he was a meddlesome opportunist that had no scruples.

The battle waged on, the Chamber was led by the friends of Francesco Crispi who, by issuing scathing dialectic blows and filibustering in the meeting hall, managed to push the government into a corner. In the end, the government realized that it could not escape and that its only option was resignation. In this manner, Crispi became Prime Minister.

At that point, Giolitti launched his counterattack.

On December 7, 1894 he crossed the semicircle of the meeting hall with very slow steps, as someone who was about to unload a serious burden onto someone else. He was a tall and thin man who often wore slim-fitting black suits. It is for this reason that he was considered a "jinx" amongst his colleagues. That day, however, he did not listen to their whispers. With a theatrical gesture, he handed over the six files that had mysteriously gone missing. Each file was divided by subject.

The largest of these files contained 102 letters that regarded Francesco Crispi and accurately described his person: an avid, ambitious man with two or three families and a lover along with a wife who cheated on him with their butler, Achille.

Giolitti begged his colleagues to ensure that the content of those letters would not be publicized, at least not those signed by Lina Crispi addressed to the butler, which explicitly stated her appreciation of his vigorous generosity.

For Crispi, newly elected Prime Minister, this was a hard blow. This was not only due to the inevitable barrage of rumors and ironic statements that would surely ensue but also because the documents clearly showed that the carelessness attributed to the Bank of Rome could directly be attributed to his pressing recommendations.

He was certain that the scandal would overwhelm him.

Crispi retained that he had no choice but to instate a mini-dictatorship. In accordance with the King, he obtained a delay for this particular Parliamentary session. Essentially, this act sealed the doors of the Chamber and thereby none of the discussions held therein could leave the hall. This provision of the Constitution had been devised but only to be implemented during a national emergency.

The reaction of the representatives was energetic but useless. Antonio Labriola stated that "Crispi fled in front of the Parliament in the exact moment that Parliament was to unmask him. He did this to save his honor." He also made a comment regarding King Umberto I: "He covered Crispi's retreat with his own irresponsibility and the king will pay for this. The Italian bourgeoisie will become a Republic. This banking scandal is the monarchy's cancer."

A few days later, the satirical newspaper *L'Asino* published a parody of the nursery rhyme written by Giuseppe Giusti:

> "To the King Log/who was given to the frogs
> We tip our hats/and give coins
> I, too, say/ that he costs us a great deal
> But it's comfortable and nice/to have a King Log
> He worries about eating/and lets others steal
> He is a King Log/who suits us quite well
> From across the marshes/one can hear people yell
> Long live the King/who lets people steal"[58]

---

[58] *L'Asino*, December 19, 1894.

Some believe that Crispi wanted to use the postponement to find a way to have Giolitti arrested, dragged to court, and, by taking advantage of some the friends he had in the magistrate, obtain a sentence that he deemed favorable. The thought must have also crossed Giolitti's mind as well because as soon as he heard about the session's delay he boarded the first train he could find bound for Berlin. He remained in Germany until the political climate changed.

For a year, Crispi was in a position to govern and he called the Chamber of Deputies into session only 11 times. With the King as his accomplice, he could make many important decisions without the need to consult the Council of Ministries. The Garibaldian hero, all faith and ideals, found himself recanting the principles he had adopted in his youth. He adopted poses and manners that were destined to become habits during the *Ventennio Nero*, during Mussolini's time.

In any event, this puppet democracy could not continue for very long. New elections were called and the electoral campaign held during the spring of 1895 was filled with violent words regarding morality.

Felice Cavallotti, who felt betrayed because in the past he had actually shared Crispi's values, was the most aggressive in reminding his despicable behavior. He wrote "open letters" to the voters and articles in widely distributed newspapers. He shouted to the masses in piazzas and compiled a series of terrifying pieces of evidence that would have destroyed any politician's career.[59]

He accused Crispi of bigamy. After having married Rosalie Montmasson in Malta, and having lived with her for 25 years, Crispi believed that this woman, the only woman amongst the one thousand Red Shirt soldiers of Garibaldi, was more suited towards hand-to-hand combat than to the salons of the aristocracy. He no longer needed her and therefore kept his distance from her with the utmost rudeness inappropriate even to use before a handmaiden. He believed that Lina Barbagallo would be

---

[59] F. Cavallotti, *La questione morale di Francesco Crispi* (Milan, 1905).

more suited to the aristocratic entertainment but in order to marry her, he had to find 5 men willing to bear witness and grant him a favor. They did: how could they deny a small favor to such a promising politician who was destined to carry out important roles.

They tried to deprive Rosalie Montmasson of the air she needed to breathe. Felice Cavallotti rendered public a note that she has written to the Prime Minister. "The man to whom I have dedicated my entire being, in all aspects of my life, aside from the mortal offense he has bestowed upon me which I will not focus on, now imposes upon me to no longer sign anything with the name that was bound to us both in sacrament and a long past. He wishes to oblige me to leave Rome and never to live wherever he chooses to live." She was reduced to a miserable state and asked to receive a license to operate a lottery booth. Could the head of the government at the time, Benedetto Cairoli, have decided to do anything before asking Crispi first? He was not even dignified with a response. Silence: refusal.

The lottery booth was not assigned.[60]

Another scandal emerged. This one had ties to Paris and had all of the elements necessary to be considered a case of international intrigue.

In France, the Society of the Panama Canal, an economic giant, had secured the favor of several representatives upon which it could count to obtain approval for the decisions in its best interests.

In that market, where even scruples had their price, the main role was occupied by a certain Cornelius Herz. He was an enterprising speculator who had ties with all those with ill-intentions that happened to have either money or power. He was identified as a dangerous corruptor and, in order to save himself from being discredited and to overturn the accusations, he believed that he could benefit from an international title. He solicited his friend Crispi to help him receive the Knighthood of the Order of San Maurizio.

---

[60] Ibid.

Said: done! One obtained the insignias he could use to act as a shield in the appropriate French circles and the other received 50,000 lira. This served as another blow to the image of an honorable politician.[61]

The final scandal made its way into the newspapers shortly before the vote was to take place.

Felice Cavallotti used an entire passage from *Don Quixote* to reconstruct a few episodes from the Bank of Rome scandal and he included a declaration made by Tanlongo.[62] "The honorable Crispi," reported the banker, "recommended I take care of the Honorable Chiara and others as far as subsidies and bills of exchange were concerned." This was an embarrassing accusation and Crispi felt obliged to respond in order to debunk any suspicions. "Tanlongo's memory deceives him," he replied. In order to appear even more convincing, he adopted the tactic of absolute negation: "I never recommended that anyone receive any discount regarding bills of exchange at his Bank."

The denial of the denial was immediate and removed any possibility of answering or at least of finding some way of justification.

A note bearing Crispi's signature was published: "The Commander Tanlongo will receive the Honorable Pietro Chiara and will treat him with the same courtesy as previously." This sounds more like an order rather than a mere recommendation.

Yet Crispi won the election by a landslide thereby demonstrating that transparency in public administration was an uninfluential factor regarding the popularity of a political leader.

Does this count today as well?

Economic analyses demonstrated that the Bank of Rome had illegally given Crispi 718,000 lira at the time. This was equivalent to 336 of his monthly salaries as Minister. Today, that would amount to approximately 7 million euro.

The institute of credit spent just as much on Crispi's entourage.

---

[61] Ibid.
[62] *Don Chisciotte*, May 20, 1895.

There were no consequences. Since he no longer had anyone who acted as an obstacle to his political actions, he governed with power that grew stronger. His credit also grew along with his power. His friends were coddled and taken care of with favors and gifts of many types while his adversaries were cast off and left to protest in a corner. Crispi's political downfall was marked by the colonial misadventure in Africa. The 1896 defeat in Adua mortified Italian nationalism and the voters made all those in power pay for it.

Part IV

Traitors and Turncoats

CHAPTER 1

GUELFS OR GHIBELLINES BUT "EITHER FRANCE OR SPAIN"

Italy remains a country of "Guelfs" and "Ghibellines": it is divided in half with each part reciprocally exchanging scowls at one another.[1] Political and cultural differences have remained intact over the course of the centuries and persecute the generations obliging them to face inexhaustible contestations. Some ongoing feuds that continue to exist: Masons versus those in favor of the Pope; those in favor of the Risorgimento and those in favor of the Church; the Unitarians versus the Federalists; the Fascists versus the Communists; those who root for FC Inter versus those who favor Juventus FC; those who are in favor of Berlusconi and those who are against him.

Possessing distinct ideological limits, in and of themselves, implies that one entertains robust convictions and has definitive certainties regarding certain matters. In reality, in the Italian character the resoluteness of "belonging" has to come to terms with an old adage: "choosing France or Spain does not matter as long as we eat." Guicciardini pronounced these words at the beginning of the 16th century when Italy was a battleground between Charles V and Francis I who fought on our turf to demonstrate their respective strength. The country seemed to be a puzzle of little states (whose main objective was to damage its neighbors as much as possible). These states offered hospitality to these large foreign armies including: logistical support, information, hotels, hospitals,

---

[1] The Guelphs and Ghibellines, two rival parties whose names are derived from two warring royal houses in Germany (Waiblingen and Welf). The sides came to be distinguished by their adherence to the claims of the emperor (ghibellines) or the pope (guelph) and impacted Italian and European politics from the 12th to the 16th century when they dissipated.

military shelters, and mechanics to repair war machines. These were offered to "either France or Spain" according to convenience.

Convictions, even those that seem to be the most deeply rooted, can lose their ground in a moment. Taking the next step, by switching sides, is just around the corner. Amongst enemies that have become friends, the process of identifying ideologies happens with great speed to the point that in a very brief time it is no longer possible to distinguish who has been there for a long time and who has just arrived. New converts in church always sit in the first pew and are always the loudest when it comes time to sing the Psalms.

The Savoys built their family fortune by playing the ambiguity game. They had placed their forts along the confines of two warring states. The forts were constructed in such a way as to allow them to fire from either side so that they could entertain the notion of switching allies at any given time. Alessandro Manzoni took note of this in his work *I promessi sposi*. "The Duke of Savoy had entered the Monferrato area and, after having taken his portion, he slowly picked away at the portion assigned to the King of Spain." In that given moment, the King of Spain was the Duke's ally, and therefore the Duke was robbing him. "Don Gonzalo was irritated by this action but feared that as soon as he raised his voice that Carlo Emanuele, who was so adept in manipulating treaties, would turn to France. Therefore he had to close one eye, tolerate everything, and be quiet." It was not long before Piedmont befriended Paris and Manzoni documented this as well. "Carlo of Nevers had decided to cede a piece of the Monferrato area to the Savoy family for 15,000 *scudi*. In a separate top-secret treaty, the Duke of Savoy ceded the Pinerolo area to France. This treaty was conducted a while later under other pretenses and as the means to perform other tricks." In the end, up until modern times, including World War II, they never ended a war with the same ally with whom they started: if it did happen it was because during the conflict they had switched sides twice.

Infidels make us angry. During electoral campaigns they promise that as soon as they reach Parliament they will do this or that, but as soon as they reach the government, that "without a binding mandate," which is upheld by the Constitution, comes into play. They can easily forget their promises and do whatever they feel is best.

Sometimes this comes down to betrayal, plain and simple, when they choose to change political party. With no sense of coherence, these politicians switch sides from the majority party to the opposition or, as it is often easier, switch from the opposition to the majority party.

This is actually not a rare occurrence. Turncoats have ancient roots and they are not even exclusively tied to this country.

"The first," joked Cossiga, "was Paul, who before becoming a saint, persecuted Christians."[2] Even Martin Luther, before rebelling against the pope, was an Augustinian monk. Winston Churchill entered politics as a conservative and then became a liberal only to return to the Tories. Gabriele D'Annunzio was elected into the Parliament with the conservatives of the Right but after only a few sessions he abandoned them. He theatrically walked across the meeting hall and exclaimed: "I am going to the Left... towards life...."[3]

Changing one's mind always carries some personal drama with it. The annals document how Lucio Colletti went from being a Communist to embracing the Forza Italia party. Mario Melloni was a Christian Democrat and then joined the Communist party and wrote an elegantly derisory article for the *L'Unità* newspaper under the pseudonym *Fortebraccio*.

Maurizio Ferrara wrote a scathing sonnet stating his opinion on the fact that his son Giuliano abandoned the Communist party to hop aboard Berlusconi's life raft. "When children take a road that you cannot travel, even if you have been stabbed with a knife, it is a lost cause to cry before a closed door."[4] But no one but he could dare to criticize his son's choice. "If Giuliano has betrayed something, then that must mean it was some-

---

[2] P. Guzzanti, *Cossiga uomo solo* (Milan, 1991).
[3] A. Spinosa, *Gabriele D'Annunzio, il poeta armato* (Milan, 1987).
[4] G.A. Stella, "Razzi e Scilipoti, quando il vitalizio fa cambiare opinione" in *Corriere della Sera*, January 22, 2013.

thing that deserved to be betrayed." Even Giuliano commended himself on his decision: "You must be at a certain level to betray."[5]

Claudio Magris observed that there was a certain way to live through a change of heart. "It depends on the type of conversion. Mary Magdalen never said anything against her former colleagues, but she also did not expect to obtain the position of President of the Virgin's Association either."[6]

The personal cases that have marked politics and history could fill an encyclopedia. For each individual's profile one could list the pros and cons as well as the extenuating circumstances and disapproval. The most sensational case in recent times concerns Sergio De Gregorio. In 2006, when he was senator, he left the Italia dei Valori Party to join Berlusconi's ranks. His "conversion" wound up in the Attorney General's Office in Naples. Antonio Razzi and Domenico Scilipoti, in the last legislature, left the Italia dei Valori party to join Berlusconi as well. They were greatly criticized in an article written by Gian Antonio Stella entitled "What Happens When One's Income Dictates One's Opinion." Despite this scathing article, the majority of these conversions concern legions of Parliament members. In the legislature that spanned from 2008 to 2013, 161 members of Parliament abandoned their original political party to seek fortune elsewhere: this is a record. To be honest, these moves were to little or to no avail. Take the President of the Chamber of Deputies, Gianfranco Fini, who was ousted in the elections held in February of 2013.

The lesson that instructed all turncoats, however, was one dictated by Camillo Benso, the Count of Cavour. He, along with his collaborator Urbano Rattazzi, managed to stage a large scale overturning of political parties. Half of the Parliament changed political party and decided to behave differently from the way the voters had elected them to act. This massive "reversal" that our school books present as an example of farsighted modernity was probably only a way to ultimately show the government's general disregard for the citizens' wishes.

---

[5] Ibid.
[6] Ibid.

Cavour was a genius of an imposter and despite his little eyeglasses he was able to see quite far and beyond more than most people. He was wider than he was tall and had a large belly that grew before him. Despite his belly, he was entirely incapable of refusing his five-course lunch. He was clearly intelligent but it was precisely because he was aware of his skill that he felt encouraged to abuse it along with his cleverness.

He was a liar of gigantic proportions. Once he was found out, the European governments no longer trusted his words: "the one thing that you would absolutely find impossible to believe is exactly that which he declares."[7]

A posthumous examination of Cavour's affirmations is as obscure as studying patristic philosophy. It did not matter whether the conversation was public or private, semi-public or semi-private. He forced himself to find the right approach to take in addressing his interlocutors in order to obtain some kind of advantage or at least to keep an argument at bay. Anyone who conversed with him, even those in disaccord with him, eventually found themselves convinced that they were on Cavour's same wavelength.

Camillo Benso, Count of Cavour, the "Father of Our Country" is largely responsible for the heaps of trouble that we have been forced to deal with from the Risorgimento onward.

Between 1849 and 1850, the Prime Minister was Massimo d'Azeglio, but it was Cavour who really ran the government. He was a meddlesome genius, a studious man with his nose always buried in papers. He was well-versed in all the most important matters and was so meticulous that he intervened in the Chamber's sessions at least 7 or 8 times on the same issue, so that he could answer to all contestations and ensure that he got the last word. This is all in spite of the fact that his voice was not very graceful and that he expressed himself in an Italian that was anything but classical.

---

[7] M. d'Azeglio, *Lettere al fratello Roberto* (Milan, 1872).

Rather than walk, he appeared to roll around gracefully by using his short, chubby legs as pivots. His face was round and puffy as though he had just eaten a stew made with wild game. He was going bald, but had tufts of blondish hair and small blue eyes. He was terribly nearsighted and required tiny eyeglasses to see.

From his appearance, one could conclude that he would have made an excellent companion with which to share a snack. Even as the Austrians were on the verge of declaring war upon Piedmont, he stated how he planned to boldly pass the time: "We've made history, now let us go and eat…"[8] His passions did not stop at restaurants, however.

He was an intriguing man who had no scruples and no remorse. He perceived diplomacy to be the art of cheating one's enemies, adversaries, and even friends whom he believed no longer served a purpose. His cynicism came naturally: "In politics, there can be no rancor and no recognition." He was not well liked by his contemporaries either. The French envoy, Duke of Guiche offered this insight: "He is a despot with no foundation: he is a man who does things only half-way."

The real patriots who dreamed of an Italy that was unclaimed put their lives on the line for what they considered "bloody boyish games."[9] In their minds, these actions should have caused insurrections but in reality they only delivered disappointment. The supporters of Mazzini attempted to cause revolutions in Milan and Lunigiana several times. Each time they lost men, weapons, and courage. Only spies increased in number, several of whom informed the police of revolutionaries and made considerable sums of money. In 1854, Giuseppe Bideschini, a leader among the revolutionaries, was actually an Austrian agent in disguise. He betrayed them all for 30,000 lira.[10]

---

[8] D. Mack Smith, *Cavour, il grande tessitore dell'unità d'Italia* (Milan, 1985).

[9] A. Venturi, *L'uomo delle bombe. La vita e i tempi di Felice Orsini, terrorista e gentiluomo* (Milan, 2009). The author refers to a phrase used in a dispatch that the police officer Domenico Buffa, serving in Genoa, wrote to the ministry in Turin to inform them that the patriots were planning something.

[10] A. Venturi, *L'uomo delle bombe.*

The patriots were impatient, violent, and careless. They continued to fight against a reality that seemed to be unchangeable. Cavour did not do this: he preferred to act upon things that were more certain.

As a minister, and by exaggerating his own abilities and pulling the rug from beneath his competitor's feet, he was able to elbow his way to become the Prime Minister. He managed to unseat D'Azeglio, who was actually responsible for introducing Cavour into the world of politics. Cavour offered him a position in his cabinet.

The "changing of the guard" did not prove to be entirely painless. Cavour had managed to sit in the chair of the Prime Minister and once he was there he organized himself by surrounding himself with an entourage of very loyal followers. A few of his more "moderate" companions in his political party no longer pleased him. He preferred to ally himself with Urbano Rattazzi's men (even though they had been elected by the opposition). So he turned a blind-eye to this small obstacle and proceeded to open the lines of communication with them. Their messages became more explicit and they often met in great secret in order to introduce their respective heads of groups. This closeness did not pass unobserved. It was clearly revealed after a series of votes held during the course of which the minority party found itself voting alongside the Cavour supporters of the majority party. It was no longer possible to deny such a coincidence.

The Honorable Ottavio Thaon of Revel decided to remove this last veil of Parliamentary hypocrisy: "I," he began in a sarcastic tone, "respect everyone's opinions, but it is precisely because I have one of my own that I will state it…. This vote clearly shows that the government has changed politics and announced to us that a new alliance has been made."[11]

"Alliance" is a word that has had a great deal of luck and was welcomed into our history with open arms. It has received numerous positive comments that protect it. It showed that the alliance between Cavour and Rattazzi and the political manipulation that had characterized it wound up being the farsighted choice of a high-ranking statesman.

---

[11] D. Mack Smith, *Cavour, il grande tessitore dell'unità d'Italia* (Milan, 1985).

In reality, "alliance" was an ugly word and, even though it might not have been explicitly stated, the adjective "carnal" seemed to be implied. A "carnal alliance" meant making love, not to one's legitimate and respectable spouse, but was the type of alliance that occurred with women of ill-repute. The words of Thaon of Revel, "a new alliance has been made," were intended to be interpreted as a heavy accusation: "You are all political prostitutes that have no shame in buying and selling one another."

Over time, the Parliament took note of the somersaults committed by those who requested the public's votes and promised to behave in a certain manner, only to change their minds and to act in ways that were completely opposite to what they had initially promised.

Agostino Depretis, years later, discovered that "transformism"[12] consisted in obtaining the support of those who had been elected into Parliament in order to criticize them. Francesco Crispi,[13] who was raised as a man of the Left but who behaved as a warmongering man of the extreme Right, believed that he had earned everyone's vote. Giovanni Giolitti,[14] after him, who had rediscovered the value of politics with no particular sense of belonging managed to stay afloat by supporting the majority, independently from who inspired him more or whose program he intended to enact. Being in the opposition didn't pay the bills and therefore was inconvenient. Positions were distributed in such a way to guarantee a loyal following. The problem, in those years, consisted in measuring out the favors so that the person elected was always left a bit vulnerable. Power was distributed similarly to the dividend of a stock. It was worth something while the company was in operation. Why would anyone want to destroy a company that freely distributed contracts, jobs, and profit?

Paolo Mieli, a journalist and director for the respectable newspapers *La Stampa* and *Il Corriere della Sera*, insists that this is truly an Italian ano-

---

[12] S. Romano, "Batta un colpo (se ci riesce)" in *Corriere della Sera*, November 12, 2010.
[13] M. Viana, *Crispi, l'eroe tragico* (Milan, 1923).
[14] N. Valeri, *Giolitti* (Turin, 1971).

maly.[15] In the rest of the world, the majority parties of the government present themselves before voters with lists of all of the things that they have managed to accomplish during their terms. If the quality of their actions is convincing enough, they proceed to obtain the necessary votes to allow them to continue their political activity. If, however, their actions are not satisfactory, the politicians are defeated and others take their place while they become the opposition. Here, they are forced to once again start over in order to once again conquer the consensus that they have lost. This happens everywhere in the world except for Italy, where alliances, though they might be in direct contrast with the programs that are to be implemented, are always made in the heart of the legislature. These choices are then ratified by the elections that follow. This has happened throughout Italy's history from the First Republic to the beginning of the second: in other words until 1994, when Silvio Berlusconi threw his hat into the ring. The only exceptions were those resulting in the dissolution of Parliament that occurred following the March on Rome by Mussolini's Fascists and during the *Mani Pulite* investigation. Mieli underlines that over the course of a century and a half, these were two extraordinary events and compared them to a human being having a heart attack.

Now, those who leave their political parties to cross over to their adversaries are considered "turncoats" and behind that word is a great deal of rancor and resentment to contemporaneously convey both disdain and disapproval. Why then should Cavour, the prince and inventor of the "turncoat" universe, be considered a mere statesman?

---

[15] P. Mieli, *L'Italia è arrivata tardi all'alternanza.* Lecture given on September 12, 2002 before the academic senate of the San Pio V University in Rome on the occasion of an *honoris causa* degree conferred in political science. The text was published by *LumsaNews.it* on September 17, 2002.

CHAPTER 2

FUGITIVES IN BLACK SHIRTS

Even Benito Mussolini who, for a Fascist, would seem to be an upstanding man, was actually a turncoat. He changed sides numerous times both in public and personal life. From Communist "Red" he converted to Fascist "Black." He went from being a "priest-eater" to marrying in Church with a large wedding. He accepted being defined as "a man of Providence." Is that enough?

He was a revolutionary who did many odd jobs in order to survive: butcher's apprentice, deliveryman for a winery, worker, and warehouse keeper. He was also unemployed at some point. It is said that his father was a great influence upon him. In reality, his father, Alessandro, was often busy with shaping iron on his anvil and between a blasphemous statement and another, was too busy to worry about his son. He was already too busy drinking and getting into fights with priests. He named his son Benito[16] (like the Mexican revolutionary Juarez) and Andrea (like Costa, a Communist from the Emilia Romagna area). He did this to be provocative.

He obtained more from Angelica Balabanov who was affiliated with the Russian intellectual elite of Trotsky and Lenin.[17] She taught him about Marx as well as washing his clothes and offering him something to eat. We have no proof of anything else though his vitality often leaves little room for doubt. She was not beautiful and had wide hips and pronounced cheekbones. But she was also not ugly, as he stated without being too subtle.

---

[16] A. Spinosa, *Mussolini, il fascismo di un dittatore* (Milan, 1989).
[17] R. De Felice, *Mussolini il rivoluzionario* (Turin, 1965).

For the rest, the future *Duce* managed by himself as he did not need any persuasion to go against the current. He was a rabble-rouser by vocation. He was even genial at times. Once, in a debate with a Protestant pastor regarding the existence of God he pulled out a watch from his pocket and exclaimed: "I shall give him two minutes to strike me down with lightning." It was his first experiment with oratorical magic. When the time was up, the crowd exploded in an applause, which rendered any following argument proposed by the theologian laughable.

Mussolini was against everything, more with his form than with his substance as could be seen by his ever-present scowl. He dealt with every issue as though it were a matter of life or death. Breaking rules, even the most insignificant ones, meant disturbing the order that the bourgeois society wanted to maintain. This was exactly what he intended to destroy. Conformity was the legacy of a society that was reactionary and bigoted. It had formalities that needed to be respected and morality that was often only a façade. The hierarchies belonged to leaders that would rather see them unchanged. Mussolini believed that a revolution should have swept all of these vestiges of the past away. This would give more space to the new generations and opportunities to the different levels of society.

He went to Monza in the company of the socialist mayor of the city.[18] He stopped before the chapel that had been built to remember the assassination of King Umberto I. He picked up a brick and etched into a nearby column the words "Monument to Bresci:" the anarchist who was responsible for killing the king. In the beginning, if he had to choose between the Savoy monarchy and those who attempted to kill them, he did not hesitate in choosing sides.

He preached free love and he dedicated himself to putting his theories into practice and began by seducing a bride who was subsequently kicked out of her house by her husband.

---

[18] I. Montanelli, *L'Italia dei notabili* (Milan, 1973).

He organized violent protests to object to the government's decision to occupy "that sandbox" known as Libia. He wound up in jail.[19]

Within the Socialist Party, the most "angry" faction was Mussolini's. He contested Bissolati because, when he was called by the King, he chose to answer. Bissolati did not present himself before the court wearing the traditional coat with tails, but rather a simple suit, however the fact that he still answered the call of the King was enough for Mussolini to request his resignation from the Party.

It was a time of great conflict. Often, the party whose members had calluses on their hands butted heads with the party of professionals who only used their hands to use pens. There were thousands of other ideological factions that were stirred for reasons that were not always clear. Often, there was actually nothing to be said, but those who chose to speak out anyway did so by yelling. Mussolini, in this respect, was unbeatable. The word *Duce* used to describe him was first used after a speech he delivered at a Socialist assembly.

He began by proclaiming himself as anti-military and was immediately declared a deserter. This happened to all men affiliated with the extreme Left. Then, in 1915, he became the head of the interventionists.[20] There was an evident break with the ideologies he had held in his youth and yet it was not as showy as it might appear. The Left remained in doubt concerning how to proceed. The most rigorous members refused to serve in the armed forces and rebelled. The anarchist newspapers *Volontà* from Ancona, *Il Libertario* from La Spezia, and *L'Avvenire Anarchico* from Pisa contemporaneously printed articles confirming the reasons behind the anti-military decision. Just the fact that it was necessary to take sides on such a matter said a great deal about the work of many revolutionaries who preferred to fight against the State, which was absolutist by definition.

---

[19] A. Spinosa, *Mussolini.*
[20] P. Alatri, *Le origini del fascismo* (Rome, 1962).

Mussolini went to the front lines and brought with him some key members of the Left such as the anarchist individualist Massimo Rocca, who used the pseudonym "Libero Tancredi." He also took Oberdan Gigli, Mario Gioda, and all those who set about to disrupt the certainties of anarchy.

The *"fasci"* were comprised of workers and they emerged from the Left. The black shirt had always been worn in the fields and factories especially in the Emilia-Romagna area. It had been chosen by farmers and workers because it did not become dirty easily and could be worn for several days. It would have been impossible to use a white shirt. Using a white shirt as a symbol meant choosing a Populist symbol and making a direct reference to the proletariat. Then the Futurist Fortunato Depero exaggerated the black shirt's importance by stating that "It is chemical-proof and appropriate for combat in war. It is elastic at home and rigid during ceremonies. It is impervious to the machine-gun and is sown with daggers and its buttons are made of bolts."

The *"Sansepolcristi,"* who in fact founded the Fascist party could not be defined as the Right or conservative for that matter. They requested universal suffrage when all those in power were more concerned with making sure that as few people as possible voted so they could maintain their position in the Parliament with as little effort as possible. They requested a republic while the aristocracy, with all of its noble titles and decorations to be worn for public events waged small wars as to who would stand closer to royalty.[21] They requested that obligatory military duty be abolished. They requested the eight-hour work day, the distribution of a company's profits amongst its workers, worker's unions within companies, civil and political liberties, and equal rights for women. The feminists were in favor of Mussolini while the ladies of the bourgeois turned their noses up to him or were actually frightened by the prospects.

In Piazza Sansepolcro there was Margherita Sarfatti, who was as red as her fiery hair and as rebellious as her curly hair. She came from a

---

[21] G.B. Guerri, *Antistoria degli italiani* (Milan, 1997).

wealthy Venetian family and could choose her destiny.[22] She wanted to write for the *Avanti* newspaper as well as for *La difesa delle lavoratrici*. Along with her was Regina Terruzzi, a teacher who had more modest origins but who believed in social promotion. There was also Ines Donati who, in 1920, was photographed in the streets of Rome as she swept to boycott the strike of the street sweepers. There was also Giselda Brebbia[23].

The people supporting the Left comprised the majority and the extremists prevailed: the Republican Armando Casalini, the revolutionary trade unionist Edmondo Rossoni, the angry socialist Ottavio Dinale, the rabble rouser from Brescia, Augusto Turati, and the anarchist from Bologna, Leandro Arpinati.

Statistics state that in those times 110 Syndicalist union headquarters, 83 workers leagues, 151 Socialist clubs, and 59 *case del popolo* were burned and destroyed. However, one cannot forget that these attacks were often guided by those who worked in those very same places in high ranking positions without exerting any influence on the politics of the country. Fascism seemed to offer them this opportunity. How could one resist?

The Left, even the official one, was very tempted by Mussolini's experiment. If it was necessary to destroy everything, well... he was doing just that. Pietro Nenni initially was beside Mussolini amongst the founders of the Fascist Party in Bologna.[24] When he saw the direction that the party was headed he fled to France. The efforts, second thoughts, and eventual abandonment and return were part of a process that has been documented in many biographies. Eucardio Momigliano who in 1946 at the end of the war published a book entitled *A Tragic and Grotesque History of Fascist Racism* was actually in Piazza Sansepolcro on March 23, 1919. Augusto Monti, the father of future dissidence in Turin, had writ-

---

[22] P.V. Cannistraro and B.R. Sullivan, *Margherita Sarfatti, l'altra donna del Duce* (Milan, 1993).
[23] V. De Grazia, *Le donne nel regime fascista* (Venezia, 1993).
[24] S. Bertoldi, *Camicia nera, fatti e misfatti di un Ventennio italiano* (Milan, 1994).

ten an articulate essay entitled "Fascism, a State Party" in 1926. The revolutionary Syndicalist Alceste De Ambris collaborated in constructing the Fascist labor unions before joining the anti-Fascists in France along with Ardengo Soffici. Ottone Rosai also participated in the Resistance.

A member of the quadrumvirate, "Michelino" Bianchi, with memories of Garibaldi and ideas that were rigorously secular, was the result of intransigent syndicalism. He had been the founder of the Syndicalist unions and he was considered to be quite meticulous in his work. He had no real physical necessities, not even at the table: a slice of salami was sufficient to feed him for the entire day. He always wore his black shirt buttoned all the way to the last button. With his pale face and white beard he resembled an accountant in mourning.

The Fascists imposed their will quickest in the territories that were considered "Red": Rovigo, Bologna, Ferrara, Pavia, and Turin. To affirm themselves in Cremona, Farinacci had to first eliminate Guido Miglioli's white cooperative associations. When Mussolini fell, those same cities that had seemed Fascist with the greatest determination revealed themselves to be in favor of the Left.

Their attitude was anti-bourgeois and disdainful. "The electrical current is strong, those who touch the Fascists face the danger of death," a popular tune recounted.

The "I don't care" slogan along with all the arsenal of skulls and crossbones came from the anarchist repertoire: "We do not care about jail, we do not care about miserable deaths."

The March on Rome, on October 28, 1922, has been recounted with anecdotes that leave one to imagine a parade of orderly legions. A march that would seem, how can we say, Fascist: with an armada of fearless men who "scaled mountains, sliding onto the plains with their daggers in their mouths and bombs in their hands." Where could we find a more appropriate comparison? Perhaps a better image to use would be that of Attila's Huns: they encountered no resistance because they were capable of destroying anyone who resisted them.

In reality, it was more like an "anarchist" walk that comprised a few thousand loyal Fascists and a large amount of odd characters that proceeded to get soaked by the rain and splashed around in the mud. It was truly a memorable effort. They merely managed to make their feet tired. They could not use their rifles if they had wanted to as they had no bullets. They crowded the taverns and inns to buy bowls of hot broth to warm their stomachs.

The most organized were the men of the provincial secretary Ricci of Carrara who placed them in a military formation and did not allow them to scatter throughout the countryside.[25] He received the congratulations of the party for his efforts. The majority of those marching were members of the proletariat. They shouted "The caves belong to the miners!" just as in the countryside they shouted, "The earth belongs to the farmers!" They were against lords and bosses that had hidden so as not to fight in the war and only now resurfaced as though nothing had happened.

No way! They would rather see everything destroyed!

The weather that day was terrible, as though God wanted to shower those people with his disapproval. Tents were haphazardly placed and poorly assembled. They were insufficient to provide any sort of shelter. Capes were too short to cover people completely. Smoke billowed from the camp sites. There was sweat and wet clothes. People wore coats from the Great War and large military overcoats along with boots and heavy shoes.

Everyone wore their black shirts but each had devised their own uniform. There were alpine hats and *bersagliere* hats and berets worn in many different ways. They were the least uniform uniforms ever to be imagined.

Those who attempted to count how many people were present believed there to be 17,000 in attendance. That number grew to 100,000 people who claimed to have traipsed in the mud on that day, as is the Italian tradition.

---

[25] G.A. Chiurco, *Storia della rivoluzione fascista* (Florence, 1936).

The quadrumvirate spent the night at the Brufani Hotel in Perugia.[26] The rooms had been diligently reserved ahead of time as though they were tourists awaiting an important event. All of the others arrived either by truck, bicycle, or on foot.

Mussolini arrived by train on the following day: when the situation was certain to have a favorable outcome to everyone's best interest. The *Duce* wanted to take his power and the king was impatient to hand it over. The script, or perhaps it was destiny, called for them to be allies.

Badoglio claimed that it would have been sufficient to kill a half-dozen men to be rid of Fascism. He was probably right, but then he began to play the part of the opportunistic mediator. Everyone immediately woke to find that those who held the power were changing. "Either France or Spain."

The masons ran to support the effort with 3 million lira.

The industrialists Pirelli and Agnelli presented themselves to manifest their satisfaction for the way things were going.

The military, following in a long tradition of the army, immediately sided with the victors.

By nightfall, Mussolini had worn more hats than a hatter but his friends and supporters had just increased exponentially. The last problem he had to face was that of presenting himself before the king for his official nomination. We know just about every last detail concerning that day but not the name of the person who lent him his suit. Truthfully, it was a little too perfect for him and actually was a little too tight around the hips.

While he was changing, the director of the Stefani Agency, Gustavo Nesti was asked "Do you have any cufflinks?[27]" Ever courteous, though a bit embarrassed, he responded, "No, your excellency, I only have one daughter." He became aware that he had misunderstood the question when he heard snickering: "Cufflinks for my shirt...."[28]

---

[26] A. Repaci, *Sessant'anni dopo* (Milan, 1982).

[27] L. Goldoni and E. Sermasi, *Benito contra Mussolini* (Milan, 1993).

[28] *Translator's note*: The Italian word *gemelli* has two meanings. It can either mean "twins" or "cufflinks" according to the context.

At the time, due to a lag in the calendar, the Russians were ahead by 12 days. The 28th of October in Rome corresponded to the 9th of November in Moscow and that was the date in which the Soviet Union celebrated the attack on the Winter Palace. It was therefore during the celebration of the 5th Anniversary of that revolution that news of Mussolini's *coup d'état* reached the USSR. Lenin was already in poor health, but during a conversation held with a delegation of Italian Communists he stated: "Only one person in Italy is capable of leading a revolution... Mussolini... You have lost him and have not been able to retrieve him."[29]

The Fascist regime was the first to acknowledge the legitimacy of the Soviet Union. Through its delegate Vorovskij, it exchanged the favor, assuring that "we have no intention of issuing any propaganda that is hostile to the Italian institutions." Beyond the curtain, they were interested in breaking through the economic blockade that the other countries were using to strangle them. Mussolini facilitated a series of contacts with businessmen in order to begin an import-export exchange that would yield both a profit.[30]

For a few months, politicians were agitated by the notion that Mussolini and Nicola Bombacci, who were old comrades that had pursued different routes, were working together to "unite the two revolutions." The fact that the official Left used a word that it considered magical, "revolution" to refer to Fascism meant that it had opened a diplomatic path for dialogue and comparison. The "third way," though perhaps it was an illusion, was the synthesis of a program that proposed finding some common points along with some divergences between Communists and Fascists.

The intellectuals that worked at the *Gironda* newspaper, the dissidents of the PSI Party, the CGIL and the PCI had often proposed erecting a bridge between the Reds and the Blacks. "If Mussolini has become Pro-Soviet why can't the Communists become Pro-Fascist?"

---

[29] G. Salotti, *Nicola Bombacci da Mosca a Salò* (Rome, 1986).
[30] A. Petacco, *Il comunista in camicia nera* (Milan, 1996).

Mussolini truly did believe in establishing a government that was open to the Left. From his notes those that he had chosen to participate in his government were: Giovanni Amendola, who was destined to take over the Ministry of National Education and the leader of the CGIL, Ludovico d'Aragona was to lead the Ministry of Labor. A "technical" ministry could have gone to Bruno Buozzi, the secretary of the FIOM, the Federation of Metallurgists. The Socialist Doctor Giulio Casalini would have been offered the Ministry of Health and the Ministry of Finance and Treasury would have been led by Ivanoe Bonomi if it remained a single ministry. If it were split into two separate ministries, the other half would have been led by the former Socialist mayor of Milan, Emilio Caldara. A ministry with no budget would have been assigned to Rinaldo Rigola, a blind socialist who was very popular. The assassination of Matteotti interrupted any prospect of dialogue and this is actually one of the strongest factors that would serve as proof that Mussolini did not order his murder.

Bombacci returned to Salò when Fascism, on paper, resumed addressing the themes of the revolutionary Left starting with imagining a Republic that should have supplanted the monarchy. Then it once again proposed the establishment of cooperatives of workers with factory labor unions and the distribution of profits.

It was Bombacci who attended assemblies and spoke to the people in a loud voice: "Comrades!" If he perceived a bit of uncertainty he would repeat: "You have understood correctly... comrades...."

But, before that time, there were 20 years that were black.

The silent majority, who knows with how much conviction, began to attend Fascist Saturdays, after-work trips, paramilitary preparations, campsites. How many people began to wear the uniform with the markings that represented the hierarchical level achieved? Even becoming the "head" of one's residential building was an honor that required effort to attain. There was something a bit contrived about being welcomed from the State at birth and to be accompanied, step by step, through to one's retirement. The people, however, seemed to believe in this notion with passion.

The historian Renzo De Felice wrote that these were "the years of consensus"[31] towards Mussolini and that the intellectual democrats revolted because it seemed like an insult to millions of Italians that claimed to have been in the opposition. They claimed... later... because earlier, their voices had certainly not been heard.

In reality, during Mussolini's regime, true opponents of the government were ultra-shy and not for their lack of abilities. They risked to be thrown in jail, confined, and even their families could suffer. Those who dared to oppose the regime faced very dire consequences.

Opponents became bolder later on, when it was no longer dangerous to be brave.

---

[31] R. De Felice, *Mussolini il Duce, gli anni del consenso* (Turin, 1974).

CHAPTER 3

THE RED SHIRTS RETURN

The black shirts were soon hidden in chests located in the attic. As soon as they became a sign of shame to the point of garnering severe consequences, they disappeared from circulation. They were quickly substituted with red ones that emerged from those same chests that had held them for many years and at the most opportune moment were returned to their rightful owners. Perhaps they were a bit dusty and slightly discolored, but only slightly.

Everyone, amidst a feeling of general resentment and with the reciprocal diffidence of the new regime, of their own history contaminated by their Fascist past, attempted to erase their past. Or at least hide it. Or at least confuse the details. Skeletons were tightly packed into closets and everyone had the impression that their closet was big enough to assure that they would not be discovered too quickly.

It was a cruel roller coaster. Hatred and rivalry were stirred up by the new Italy. Many aspired to an immediate purification that was viewed as a necessity in order to earn the right to obtain a new democratic passport. There were those who eagerly bought up deplorable pasts in the shadow of Mussolini: they risked passing quickly from the accuser to the accused. The archives, or often only a handful of rumors, were sufficient to provide enough stories and indiscretions from which it seemed that no one was completely safe.

In the end, who had not asked for a favor? Who had not received some sort of assistance?

In the halls of newspaper offices, universities, theaters, cinemas, and in the art world there were many whispers alluding to favors large and small that various people had received. There were allusions regarding mediocre compromises and humiliating weaknesses.

Who had the credibility to issue badges of merit?

Concetto Marchesi spoke out against "the vileness of intrigue"[32] of those intellectuals that had frequented the labyrinths beneath the Fascist current. They sought in Communism the "miraculous pool where lepers bathed and emerged purified." Yet even such a stern censor could not rest too easily. Even he had become the target of many doubts and insinuations regarding his compromising oaths, enrolment in Fascist academies, the Fascist Party membership cards and documents that went missing, but were never completely canceled. This was embarrassing.

Therefore, who could wear the garb of the "purifier" if even the most eligible candidate ran the risk of needing to be "purged"? Two men posed themselves this question: Ernesto Rossi and Gaetano Salvemini. During the Fascist regime they had come to know jail and exile and therefore they were beyond any suspicion. "In Florence," they replied with some contempt, "they say that those who salute with their fists closed do so in order to ensure that their Fascist pins do not slip from their fingers."[33]

In most cases, people went to great lengths to bury a past that no one wanted to remember. Erasing collective memory was convenient to all, even to those who had the most to gain by pinpointing blame.

Mirella Serri, professor of contemporary Italian literature at the University of Rome, dedicated years of research before writing a book that was appropriately titled: *The Redeemed: The Intellectuals Who Lived Twice 1937-1948*.[34] First, these individuals wore the Fascist uniform, if they were not already on Mussolini's payroll. They were convinced Fascists. Then they materialized under the protective flags of the hammer and sickle. Conversion was favored and encouraged by Palmiro Togliatti, the secretary of the PCI Party. It was he who, in order to collaborate with the newspaper *Rinascita* together with the leaders of the political party, involved those intellectuals that had gravitated around Giuseppe Bottai,

---

[32] P. Bucarelli, *1944 Cronaca di sei mesi* (Rome, 1977).

[33] E. Rossi and G. Salvemini. Edited by M. Franzinelli, *Dall'esilio alla Repubblica. Lettere 1944-1957* (Turin, 2004).

[34] M. Serri, *I redenti. Gli intellettuali che vissero due volte 1938-1948* (Milan, 2005).

who was the mastermind behind the journals *Primato* and *Critica Fascista*. It is worthwhile to note that during those twenty years of the Fascist Regime, there were no "soft" publications. The publications represented the roughest and most uncompromising view of orthodox Fascism. After the publication of the "Manifesto of the Racial Scientists," published on July 14, 1938, Bottai had stated that the racial laws were one of the most important conquests made by Mussolini's regime.[35]

Togliatti also called the writer Sibilla Aleramo to collaborate with the newspapers of his party. During the 1930s, she had been the lover of Enrico Emanuelli, a writer for the Fascist newspaper *Primato*. In 1933 she had received a salary from Mussolini that amounted to 1000 lira per month. She offered her contribution to the PCI member Carlo Bernari and wrote in Bottai's newspaper until January 1, 1943, by publishing a serial novel.[36] To ensure that her conversion to the Left would be even more credible, Bernari founded a publishing house, aptly named *Nuova Biblioteca* and proposed the complete works of Antonio Gramsci. When it came time for the leaders of the Communist party to offer their approval, Nello Ajello criticized his action as "a little pathetic"[37] and Togliatti hemmed and hawed until nothing was ultimately done. What did he care about Gramsci anyway?

Cesare Zavattini, the father of Neorealism joined the ranks of Leftist anti-Fascists. He signed his "literary whims" published in the *Primato* simply as "za."[38]

Renato Guttuso and Domenico Purificato, besides being illustrators, often were art critics in the pages of Communist newspapers. Afro, Mirko, and Ernesto Treccani published their drawings in *Rinascita*.

---

[35] G. Bottai, *Politica fascista della razza*, in «Critica fascista», August 1, 1938.
[36] C. Bernari, "I loro passi e le loro voci" in *Primato*, July 1 and 15, August 1 and 16, 1941.
[37] N. Ajello, *Intellettuali e PCI. 1944-1958* (Rome-Bari, 1979).
[38] C. Zavattini, *Cinquant'anni e più. Lettere 1933-1989*. V. Fortichiari, ed. (Milan, 1995).

In Togliatti's new court, the new and old indistinctively were mixed together. There were old comrades whose faith had been tested and had been party members for many years. Some of them had even been to jail or persecuted. There were also "newer" members that had been directly recycled from the Fascist regime.

It is comprehensible that there might be some bad blood between these two factions.[39] How is it possible to not make a distinction between those who were authentically anti-Fascist from the beginning and those who were "coffee pot rebels" who had only "brewed" and voiced notions of discordance in the last months of the war?

There were many arguments that addressed this problem throughout the Party's ranks. What should the requisites be in order to obtain admission in the ranks of the hammer and sickle? Palmiro Togliatti, however, did not want to listen to any of these arguments. He was working very hard to retrieve the younger generations of Fascists. It was said that he was not worrying too much about the present but rather was working towards the future. [40] He was setting up the framework for a very powerful "amnesty" that was destined to close matters of the past that would have been handed to historians in order to leave the politicians in peace.

Gaetano Azzariti, president of the Racial Court, an infamous institution, became a strong collaborator of Migliore, at the Ministry of Justive (after having been the Minister of Justice under Badoglio).

A dispersion of Fascists occurred in the universities, banks, and public administration. Intellectuals and professionals that had previously held often more than one title during the time of the Fascist Regime were being "saved" and "rehabilitated" by the Communists. *The Times*[41] and *The Economist*[42] took note of "a wide and growing presence of former Fascists in the Communist Party."

---

[39] G. Bocca, *Palmiro Togliatti* (Bari, 1977).
[40] Ibid.
[41] *The Times*, August 7 and December 30, 1944.
[42] *The Economist*, October 30, 1944.

A group of former Fascists united around the newspaper *Pensiero Nazionale*. They were united by the stance held by Stanis Ruinas, a Sardinian writer who believed the earliest form of Fascism, the one that advocated a social Republic. He believed this initial thought was betrayed by those who ultimately surrounded Mussolini. Fascism, according to him, was originally a Leftist, revolutionary movement. Therefore, there should be no trouble in finding common ground with those Communists who hoped for a revolution. His opinion was shared by a growing number of intellectuals that had rigorously served in the social Republic of Salò. These included: General Emilio Canevari, a man who had been close to General Rodolfo Graziani; General Nemesio Beltrame; Rear-Admiral Ferruccio Ferrini, who was the Undersecretary for the Marines; the "black" syndicalist Silvio Galli; Fausto Brunelli; and the journalists Aniceto Del Massa and "Berto" Ricci. There were also some vestiges from the 10th Fleet of the MAS: Alvise Gigante and Giampaolo Testa (who were both sons of hierarchs) along with Spartaco Cilento and Luca Scaffardi.

These were all people who had held and maintained important roles through the very last hours of the Fascist regime (arguably the most violent and bloody moment). They could have all therefore expected to be put on trial so that they could be "purged" quite soon. They wound up supporting the PCI and were protected by the Communists. In some cases, they were even financed by those same Communists. They became known as "Red Fascists" or "Black Shirt Communists."[43]

Giancarlo Pajetta maintained rapport with the magazine *Pensiero Nazionale*. Initially, he moved cautiously, but as time went on, his actions became more overt.

In an editorial published in the *Unità* newspaper entitled "Reconquering Italy's Sons," he stated that he did not believe it was possible to abandon those "who were drawn to the ranks of Graziani's army by terror, acquiescence, or misinterpretation." He continued: "We really have

---

[43] P. Buchignani, *Fascisti rossi. Da Salò al Pci; la storia sconosciuta di una migrazione politica 1943-55* (Milan, 1988).

no reason to act cruelly toward thousands and thousands of youths who could stand to learn something from honest work and hard labor."[44] It was a matter of "opening a line of credit" that would allow a good number of Fascists, by now former Fascists, to reach the Communist headquarters to ask for membership in the new party.

The PCI bolstered the number of its members and played all of its best cards to conquer the majority vote in the electorate (and therefore the government). Those who had small or large sins to be pardoned chose to embrace the Red flag because they offered better and stronger protection. Under the Red tent, the barriers were growing more resistant.

Though this was not true for everyone, and not in the same manner either.

Pierluigi Battista examined several cases in order to discover any blatant injustices.

Massimo Bontempelli, one of the most prestigious intellectuals during the regime, did not deem it sufficient to become a Communist and be elected to the Senate in 1948 under the Leftists. He received a condemnation from the Court of "Purification" and it declared him ineligible for his position as he had written "books and scholarly texts of Fascist propaganda." He was forced to leave his position. Yet Bontempelli, at the University of Florence, had refused to take the place of Professor Attilio Momigliano, who had been removed due to anti-Semitic discrimination. He demonstrated a degree of personal coherence and yet he was forced to face an extraordinarily harsh sentence. Other professors, instead, did not hesitate to take the place of other Jewish professors that had been removed from the halls of academia, yet they did not have to face any trial and we have no proof that they ever had to face any punishment of any sort.

Why was there such disparity in passing judgment?[45]

---

[44] G. Pajetta, "Riconquistare i figli all'Italia" in *l'Unità*, September 15, 1945.
[45] P. Battista, *Cancellare le tracce. Il caso Grasse il silenzio degli intellettuali italiani dopo il fascismo* (Milan, 2006).

Giorgio Levi Della Vida, one of 12 professors out of 1,200 who refused to pledge loyalty to the regime, was fired from the university. He was forced to protest loudly, and for a very long time, in order to obtain the financial compensation he deserved, which had accumulated over the years from the time he was fired from his tenured position.[46]

It seems as though the wheels of fortune moved with an improbable and incomprehensible rhythm.

Curzio Malaparte attempted to join the Great Red Church, but found the door closed. The only thing left for him to do was to vent his anger with his bitterly ironic writing. "Italy, therefore, will be nothing but a Fascist Italy, dressed in as many uniforms as there are anti-Fascist parties." Davide Lajolo was a Communist but he had "previously frequented Salò for a long time." Carlo Muscetta, an editor for the *Unità* newspaper had been "a humble servant of the servants of Mussolini." Titta Rosa, with all of his anti-Fascism, "had written a book on Balbo that was filled to the brim with rhetoric." Moravia "requested to be accepted by the Fascists but was rejected... he then proceeded to use his brother's death in Tobruk as leverage...."[47]

Explicit contestations carried the mark, that was both extreme and contrasting, of all those who complained that the Resistance had been "betrayed" by the partisans and who were disgusted by the lack of coherence by the vast amounts of people who had denied convictions that up until a few moments prior had fiercely advocated. To the extreme Left, it seemed as though all of the efforts to "free" Italy had been weakened if they were not completely in vain. It was useless to hope in a "new" nation. Those people who had been in power up until that point continued to govern simply by changing the color of their shirt.

On the other side, the nostalgic people that proudly, and obstinately, clung to the past were horrified by the arrogance with which the former Fascist officials and soldiers converted their biographies by opportunisti-

---

[46] Ibid.
[47] F. Perfetti, "Contra il fascismo dell'antifascismo" in *Nuova Storia Contemporanea*, May-June 2000.

cally leaving a few passages out to emphasize others. How could they do such a thing? Had they not shared these experiences together? How could they forget? To them, it seemed to be a shameless attitude. Loyalty to the side that has lost was a motive for pride. The new anti-Fascists that, sometimes fumbled in watering down their pasts as Fascists, found themselves ridiculed by anyone who happened to find a photo, a declaration, or even a detail of their Fascist past.

Nino Tripodi, a director in the MSI who had frequented the Fascist legions from which many high-ranking anti-Fascist officials emerged, became highly specialized in carrying out a crusade against turncoats. He published two books: *Fascist Italy, Stand Up*, and *Intellectuals under Two Flags*. They were constructed as overt comparisons of people's works prior to the Fascist era and after it.

For example: a phrase written by Arturo Carlo Jemolo during the regime was placed next to another written in an anti-Fascist style. An excerpt written by Mario Alicata during the regime compared to another addressing a similar topic but with completely different opinions written during the Republic. This comparison was executed on the works of many people, including: Emilio Cecchi, Salvatore Quasimodo, Salvatore Rosai, Alberto Savinio, Romano Bilenchi, Walter Binni, Elio Vittorini, Cesare Zavattini, and practically all of the symbols of Italian culture.[48]

Not even Professor Norberto Bobbio was spared, though he had the intellectual honesty to admit his faults. He was a member of the Fascist Party and upon receiving a tenured position in the university when he was 30 years old he had sworn loyalty to the party during the war. There are letters that were written and signed by him in which he had written exhortations to Mussolini and other officials. He was rightly ashamed of these letters.[49]

---

[48] N. Tripodi, *Intellettuali sotto due bandiere. Il conformismo della cultura* (Rome, 1981).

[49] M. Veneziani, "Bobbio, i fascisti e i veleni invecchiati" *Il Giornale*, December 1, 2012.

Yet, with a few individual exceptions and going beyond the feuding Left and Right sides that were nostalgic for the fight to survive beyond their values, everything else returned to normalcy under the veil of conformity.

Remembering is a tiresome activity.

This was true then and it is true now. Massimo Coco emphasizes this thought. He is a famous violinist who travels the world and is invited to play at the most prestigious venues. He is the son of Francesco Coco, a prosecutor who was murdered by the *Brigate Rosse* in Genoa on June 8, 1976. He wrote a book to express his frustration and to pose a question. "For crying out loud," he asks, "where have you hidden your anger?"[50] He addresses several victims who have become VIPs: in other words those who have undergone a series of steps of "do-good removal" that would allow for "a public re-elaboration of grief" to allow for a "cathartic finale." He wanted to join another party, though it was an extreme minority: the "non-forgiving" party. He claims the right to be filled with rancor and to nurture the desire for vengeance, which he believes is only human. "Who has made you experts on being victims?" Coco asks. "I do not mean to stretch out the night any further but I dream of illuminating it with the light of truth and justice." He also states, "I do not have the right to forgive in my father's place. Who has given you this right?"[51]

---

[50] M. Coco, *Ricordare stanca. L'assassinio di mio padre e le altre ferite mai chiuse. Dal figlio della prima vittima delle Brigate Rosse un atto d'accusa contra l'uso mediatico della memoria* (Milan, 2012).
[51] G. Sallusti, *"Mio padre ucciso dalle Br. Io non perdono. Massimo Coco, figlio del Procuratore trucidato nel 1976: sono libero di odiare e, anzi, rivendico il mio desiderio alla vendetta"* in *Il Giornale*, November 25, 2012.

Part V

Justice… Justice…

CHAPTER 1

THE TASTE OF "SUGAR CUBES" IN THE TOBACCO SHOP SMOKE

The scandal of the sale of the tobacco monopoly happened in 1868. Luigi Federico Menabrea was Prime Minister. He was a general in the Savoy army and fiercely loyal to King Victor Emanuel II whom he had assisted on the field. Luigi Cambrai-Digny was the Minister of Finance. He descended from a noble French family that had moved to Tuscany and was a great landowner. He was the government's "strongman."

These were times when Italy's finances were in the red. The price of the wars of independence, the devastating military campaigns, and the transfer of the capital city, first to Florence and then to Rome, had delivered heavy blows to the already fragile condition of the State's coffers. A poor management of public funds did not help either. At that time, public funds did not produce what they were supposed to because they were actually dispersed into thousands of rivulets that served many opportunists. Never mind the spending review's savings, costs continued to inflate, causing such a high debt that Italy was on the verge of bankruptcy. Banks were no longer in the condition to offer loans to the State because the risk of losing their investments was considered high. Therefore, the government hypothesized selling the rights to their monopoly on tobacco, thereby privatizing an entity that was wealthy and profitable to recuperate some financial autonomy and receive a few million lira in liquidity.

This operation turned into a fraud of colossal proportions.[1]

The State's tobacco factories, despite the presence of certain pockets of parasites and the fact that they were burdened by wastefulness that can easily be imagined, actually yielded a profit. Therefore, purchasing them

---

[1] L. Levi Sandri, *Il giallo della Regìa* (Rome, 1983).

would have been a good deal. The banker Balduino was the most enter-prising in this effort and took advantage of the situation. He put together a group of interested investors and he must have been terribly convincing because in a few weeks he was able to present an offer that was sufficient-ly credible. The State would have immediately made 180 million lira and from the following January, for twenty years, the new company would have managed the tobacco monopoly. The agreement was signed with exceptional speed on June 23, 1868. However, in order for it to become valid, it required Parliament's vote.

The government called the Chamber of Deputies into session on the 4th of August, perhaps betting on the fact that either the sea or the moun-tains would lure the representatives away from their institutional duties.[2] Instead, vacations were placed on hold. Everyone was present and partic-ipated in the debate with conviction to the point that the discussion went on for four days and was as heated as the temperature outside. The tradi-tional Parliamentary alliances split. The men of the Left who deferred to Antonio Mordini were in agreement with the government. Many of those on the Right, however, contested the decisions of the majority party to which they belonged. Giovanni Lanza, the President of the Chamber, abandoned his position of impartiality in order to speak as "a simple rep-resentative" and to contest governmental decisions. The very person who was responsible for the great cover-up of the railway investigation found himself as the prince of morality in the Tobacco Affair. Perhaps it was for this reason, though without sparing any criticism, that he did not let himself get carried away with oratorical rhetoric. He concluded by offer-ing this observation: "Either the government must suppress monopolies or keep them for itself."

Minister Cambrai-Digny presented himself before the Chamber of Deputies to illustrate the need to rationalize the tobacco business' pro-cesses of production in such a way to render them more functional and efficient. There was a certain haughtiness in his manner of speaking as

---

[2] Archivio storico della Camera dei deputati, parliamentary proceedings, 1868.

he addressed the Parliament. He cited numerous examples of poor management and, in the end, was resolute in indicating one possible solution: assigning the management of the tobacco business to an association of capitalists. They would "be free from many ties and traditions of the government" and would be able to rapidly intervene "to eradicate any abuses and proceed to make decisive changes." Only a private group of investors could do such a thing because "since their interests would be at stake" they would be in the condition to implement "those standards and systems that would more easily create a better product."[3] In the solemn atmosphere of the Parliament, the minister expressed himself using exactly these terms: the tobacco business needed only simple, minor adjustments. Imagine if the interventions were considered complicated or would require who knows what specific abilities. The Minister of Finance highlighted that the instruments that needed to be applied actually derived from elementary intuition: the changes were easy if not downright trivial. How could one not nurture the suspicion that, behind this operation, there were not professional opportunists?

The corruption was in fact methodical and widespread yet, in spite of this fact, the majority party held on by only 19 votes.

It was too evident that behind the Parliament's decisions there were illegal favors, promises made, and bribes measuring in the millions of lira.

At that time, bribes were called "sugar cubes." The Minister of Finance Cambrai-Digny must have tasted one. The future Minister of Justice, Michele Pironti, destined to be a protagonist in the next chapter of the affair, received one as well. As far as the part that personally affected King Victor Emanuel II, we actually know the amount: 6 million lira.[4]

In all, around 50 million lira were distributed in varying amounts. These were sufficient to satisfy about a hundred members of Parliament.

Felice Cavallotti, who had earned himself the title of "the bard of democracy" for his battles waged for the sake of morality, picked up his pen

---

[3] Archivio storico della Camera dei deputati, parliamentary proceedings, 1868.
[4] L. Levi Sandri, *Il giallo della Regia.*

and wrote a series of articles in the *Gazzetta di Milano* that gave some weight to the heaviest suspicions. The first names of those presumed to be corrupt appeared only on the pages of the *Gazzetino rosa*:[5] Honorable Giuseppe Civinini from Pistoia, who initially sided with Crispi and the Left but then moved to the more moderate end of the political spectrum; Raimondo Brenna, a representative and the director of the newspaper in Florence, *La Nazione*; Brenna's brother-in-law, Paul Fambri. These suspicions were poisonous and the doubts instilled were infamous.

Did the magistrate seek to open an investigation in order to obtain some clarity?

Civinini and Brenna took legal action against those Lombard newspapers and dragged them to court where the newspapers were found guilty of slander through printed media from the magistrate.[6] Judicial victory, however, was worse than defeat because during the course of the trial, too many circumstances reinforced the newspapers' conviction that those two gentlemen were anything but clean.

The element that became the center of attention concerned the friendship between Civinini and a certain Salvatore Tringali, who had received a considerable share in the privatization of the tobacco industry: 1 million lira. How was it possible that a "nobody" like Tringali could come upon such a vast sum of money? How could one not suspect that he merely lent his name to someone else and that that certain someone was not Civinini? The magistrates did not ask too many questions and made their judgments by taking into consideration only the most obvious details.

The Chamber, however, began to tremble. On June 2, 1869 a representative of the extreme Left, Giuseppe Ferrari, presented the request for the formation of a committee to conduct a Parliamentary investigation. This would be to put an end to the rumors, misunderstandings, and issue blame where it was due. There were too many ambiguous characters, according to his reconstruction of the facts. There were too many doubts,

---

[5] *Gazzettino rosa*, August 8, 1868.
[6] The sentence was pronounced on September 30, 1868.

starting from the fact that the tobacco shares were worth 152 lira before the agreement and they skyrocketed to 650 lira at the moment the privatization took place. The increment was so large as to warrant the suspicion of fraud.

The debate continued for days. It was difficult to predict the outcome.

On June 5, 1869, a turning point took place. From the benches of the Left rose the representative Cristiano Lobbia. He was a broad-shouldered man who was two meters tall and had the hands of a man who was used to manual labor. He was an officer under Garibaldi in Sicily and he fought like a lion in Meri and Milazzo where he earned his captain's stripes. Surely, he was one of those who had imagined a different Italy than what was eventually constructed. The new kingdom had led to disappointment. In 1866, when the Third War of Independence broke out, he returned to the army to ensure that the Veneto region would join the tricolor flag. Then, he was elected a representative and in Parliament he was assigned to the commission that dealt with matters of war. No one ever doubted his honesty and yet the bizarre course of history allowed him only to be remembered for the shape of his hat: a *lobbia* or Homburg style hat with a starched brim that was the width of a palm. In his native town of Asiago, there is a town square named after him but no one seems to know why.

"I solemnly announce," he began, "that I am in possession of declarations by witnesses, that are above all exceptions and that refer to profits made in the tobacco affair. These declarations have been made legal by the seal of a public notary. They are enclosed in these files that I hold in my hand." With little drama, but perhaps with a pinch of haughtiness, he turned towards the left with his hand raised to show the files. With the finger from his other hand he pointed to the wax seals. "When you nominate a commission to conduct the investigation," he promised, "it will be my duty to present them with these papers and I personally will arrive in the company of the witnesses to be examined."

Whispers became a rumble and on one side they turned into shouts while on the other they turned into applause worthy of any stadium.

The majority saw the specter of a thunderous, dishonorable defeat looming on the horizon. The opposition, on the other hand, felt like they had received a much needed boost.

Prime Minister Menabrea intervened to declare himself contrary to even considering Lobbia's action. This says a great deal about the level of agitation that was encircling the ministries, which, having accepted to favor any number of schemes, did not yet understand how to avoid getting themselves into trouble if not by blatantly denying the evidence.

Ruggiero Bonghi attempted to speed up the process of the investigation by requesting that the names of the persons involved be revealed to the public and that, at the very least, those documents be made immediately available to Parliament.

"Nope!" Lobbia did not even need any time to think before making his reply. "Some other very important documents have already gone missing from the Chamber's archives in the past. I intend to keep these myself..."[7]

The representatives had no alternatives. They unanimously voted on the investigation committee. Nine members were selected including Giuseppe Zanardelli[8] the future Prime Minister. Even in this case with a *notitia criminis* of this size, did the king's lawyers intervene? They washed their hands of the matter.

The Parliament's investigation began its winding course, often slowed down by often useless bureaucratic measures. It was often hindered by such a large number of expedients that were in many cases mere formalities.

Lobbia, on the other hand, began to pay for his courage. Two days later, on a night with a new moon that was heavy with humidity, the rep-

---

[7] Archivio storico della Camera dei deputati, parliamentary proceedings, 1869.

[8] The other members of the committee were: Giuseppe Pisanelli, Ferdinando Andreucci ,Giuseppe Biancheri, Benedetto Cairoli, Salvatore Calvino, Michele Casaretto, Nicolò Ferracciù, Mariano Fogazzaro.

resentative was walking between the Chamber and a journalist friend's home when he was attacked by an assassin with a knife. The representative had turned from Via Sant'Agostino on to Via dell'Amorino. An unknown man was waiting for him, hiding in the shadows. The man was rapid and precise but was unable to complete his duty purely by chance. His knife blade pierced Lobbia's leather wallet that was filled with papers, personal documents, a few banknotes, and four photos of his parents. The initial blow did not meet its mark but the assassin made another attempt. The designated victim reacted and grabbed the assassin's arm. He fell to the ground and dragged his attacker down with him. It was a terrible struggle. A second blow came from the assassin. It pierced Lobbia's side and a third blow injured him quite seriously on the head. The representative, however, was an old fighter and was able to grab a revolver that he had in his pocket. He was able to fire two shots. The sound of the weapon aroused the neighborhood's attention and at that point the assassin had no choice but to flee.[9]

The wounded man received tons of letters of solidarity while he was being treated for his injuries. Throngs of protestors gathered in the squares to shout his name and shout, "Down with political cliques!" The people had understood perfectly well that the reason for his attack was closely related to his speech given in Parliament a few days prior.

Garibaldi wrote him a message: "Dear Lobbia! You were respected by enemy fire when you fought on the battlefield. You almost fell victim to the dagger of an assassin because you were disdainful in the face of Italian shame and the morality of those who should be setting moral examples for the people." Newspapers at the time reported that "in Florence, ill-will was brewing." The people were upset. "From conversation to conversation," reported one journalist, "rumors were growing stronger that said that there were hired assassins that were ready to kill for money any who dared to challenge these powerful bankers."[10]

---

[9] "L'aggressione a Lobbia" in *La Nazione*, June 18, 1869.
[10] Ibid.

The Minister of Internal Affairs, Ferraris, was obliged to respond in Parliament to a series of requests for information. He reported the events in full detail and denounced the crime with vehemence. He denied the rumor that the authors of such a crime could be corrupt policemen.[11] In truth, the executors of Lobbia's assassination attempt were men of the secret service who today would be considered "deviant." At this time they resided in Palazzo Riccardi.[12]

The attack kicked the committee's work into high gear and, on the 16th of June, it held its first meeting. Lobbia, who was in the hospital, could not participate. Instead, Crispi presented himself and accused Civinini, Brenna, and Fambri, the very same men mentioned by the *Gazzettino rosa* but this time with a document that did not leave any margin of doubt. He presented a message written by Brenna to his brother-in-law Fambri. "Dear Paul, suspend any negotiations you may have concerning our share. Today, I spoke with the banker Balduino and I made our situation clear. He anticipates that we will receive a handsome profit and that therefore it is no longer convenient for us to sell anything. Therefore, send me this letter and let us see to it that we earn some nice money. I have established a direct daily communication with Balduino. Say hi to Rosina for me. Please write. *Ciao*."[13]

It was a member of Brenna's household staff that stole the letter to hand it over to a representative of the Left (probably Francesco Cucchi, one of the *Mille* soldiers) who in turn had given it to Cristiano Lobbia. Crispi had taken it from Lobbia taking advantage of the fact that he was in the hospital. When Lobbia presented himself before the Parliament's committee, he no longer had the most damning piece of evidence. He had all the documents that demonstrated a lowly, immoral business deal, but all of these were insufficient to justify his previous intervention a few days prior.

---

[11] Archivio storico della Camera dei deputati, parliamentary proceedings, 1869.
[12] A. Viviani, *Servizi segreti italiani (1815-1985)* (Rome, 1985).
[13] Archivio storico della Camera dei deputati, parliamentary proceedings, 1869.

Lobbia had frightened the corrupt and the corruptors. He let others believe that he held in his possession more than he really had. They, however, had tried to make amends by sealing his mouth forever. After having verified the papers he had, they changed strategy. They set in motion a series of actions to discredit that gentleman and to try to pass him off as a poor, unserious man with a vivid imagination. The work done by Michele Pironti, the Minister of Justice was instrumental and decisive. He put pressure on the prosecutors and the magistrates of half the country. He skillfully managed to offer a mix of bribes and threats in order to turn the accuser into the accused.

The Public Prosecutor of the Court of Florence, Marabotti, was in charge of handling the assassination attempt on Via dell'Amorino. There were two key witnesses. Angelo Fabbrucci, who was a customs tax employee whose home was near the crime scene, heard the shouts and the echo of the first shot but saw little or nothing. He only saw the shadow of the man who fled. His description of the assailant was entirely generic: "medium stature, black beard, stocky build." The other witness was a young man from Cremona, Mario Scotti, who was an employee of the Italia Alta railways who rented a room from Fabrucci. This man must have seen far more than what he cared to say because it frightened him to the point of death. For a few days he continued to present himself at work but flinched at any sudden movements. He walked with his back towards the wall as though trying to hide himself. He even avoided greeting his colleagues. He was then struck with a fever that confined him to bed where, in a delirious state, he repeated, "I will not say anything." Fabrucci's wife tended to him "with hosts and several disgusting insects that popular superstition believes can cure jaundice." Scotti did not heal and did not recover. In two days, his funeral preparations were made. Was he poisoned? His mother, in a letter written to his relatives was not hesitant to state that she believed this to be the case. Even the magistrate must have nurtured some measure of doubt because he ordered an autopsy on the body to attempt to understand what had actually happened.[14]

The posthumous examination, however, never took place. Marabotti's superiors sustained that the funeral could not be delayed and with a peremptory order, they revoked the request. Precisely because that young magistrate showed willingness to meddle in affairs that were irrelevant, and therefore demonstrating that he was inadequate to meet the needs of justice he was removed from the case. In his place, they called Count Adolfo De Foresta, who knew the ways of the world and was therefore capable of making a considerable contribution to the investigation.

The events, according to the new magistrate, had gone quite differently. The episode was deemed not as an attack but rather a well-staged occurrence. There was a fake assassin, complacent witnesses, and instances that were purely invented. In other words, the whole thing was staged to garner favor in the public opinion.

The Public Prosecutor had the gall to support the accusation of simulation of a crime in the court. The judges had no shame in accepting this thesis and therefore condemned Lobbia to a year of prison. His journalist friend and the people who had sought to help him when he was wounded were all held responsible as accomplices and were condemned, though they managed to squeak by with minor sentences. What a scandal.

Once the sentence was pronounced, the magistrates who had acted according to indication received promotions, notes of merit, and access to the salons of the political elite.

At the same time, in Milan, a judge that had absolved 22 people who had protested in favor of Lobbia by staging a sit-in was removed from his position. They were supposed to be condemned for "disrupting public order." The acquittal was immediately reversed and was reformulated to include a sentence that would have discouraged anyone who chose to

---

[14] S. Turone, *Corrotti e corruttori dall'unità d'Italia alla P2* (Bari, 1984).

follow their example.[15] The slandering campaign against Lobbia came to know another disgusting turn of events.

On the evening of August 22, 1869, Lobbia walked through the streets of Florence with his trusted journalist friend, Antonio Martinati. He noticed at one point that he was being followed by a person whom he did not know and who continued to look at him with insistence. He thought that someone might be following him, though not in a very skillful manner. Since his wounds were still healing from his previous attack, he did not have the quick wits to properly evaluate the alleged spy.

When he came upon two *carabineri*, he informed them of his identity and recounted his suspicions. The *carabineri* carried the man away. Two days later, a trial was held that was well-attended by many journalists that had been called ahead of time. The man, Giuseppe Lai, was a Franciscan friar that had been expelled from the order because he was a homosexual. The transcripts read that "he was dedicated to the practice of sodomy." He declared that he had followed those men because he believed that he believed the younger of the two shared his tastes and that he wanted to propose an "affectionate" encounter. It goes without saying that this episode was perfectly staged. If the friar had truly been a harmless seducer he would have immediately stated his intentions to the *carabineri* and the matter would have been resolved without much ado. Instead, Giuseppe Lai waited to make his affirmations in public in order to cause as much scandal as possible and thereby exposing the representative to an embarrassing situation that rendered him ridiculous. "You know," he stated before Judge Cantini, "when I am out alone at night, I stare at men."[16]

At the end of the nineteenth century, homosexuality was an act that was punishable by law. Aside from the penal code, it was a social scar that people were careful to avoid. Certainly, a man who had been defrocked and was now known by the police had nothing more to lose. The

---

[15] Ibid.

[16] "L'affare Lobbia-Lai" in *La Nazione*, August 29, 1869.

trap consisted in involving Cristiano Lobbia and ruining his reputation with a story that was ambiguous. A suspicion regarding his virility was equivalent to a condemnation with no further appeals possible. The movements proposed by Minister Pironti were working perfectly. This second episode would have served to complete the moral lynching of that poor man.

In the end, they accused him of stealing the letter written from Brenna to Fambri and they proceeded to call for a trial for theft. This last passage failed those in power because they found a magistrate that was capable of standing his ground.

Borgnini, the King's lawyer, recognized the absurdity of this blatantly persecutive accusation. He immediately signed the acquittal act. His decision was one that was not to be taken for granted. His superior, Avet, led him to believe that if he maintained a certain disposition, it could help his career. The young magistrate disobeyed the wishes of the hierarchy and he listened to his conscience. The head of his office immediately invited the magistrate, on order by the Minister, to request two months leave. This would have been enough time to find an alternate solution and to recuperate the trial. Borgnini replied by submitting his resignation. He hung his lawyer's robes on a hook and chose to change profession.[17]

The posthumous revelations issued by a group of judges from Lucca regarding Lobbia were useless. When the courts recognized that the accusations against the man were false and that the issues he had raised regarding the businessmen who had "hired" government members were true, it was too late. The Honorable representative had already died from rage and heartbreak.

In the meantime, the scandal of the privatization of the tobacco industry had already been forgotten

History's pages do not speak of the scandal concerning the privatization of the tobacco monopoly. Therefore those who study are not in any condition to find documents regarding the bribes that were paid in order

---

[17] S. Turone, *Corrotti e corruttori dall'unità d'Italia alla P2.*

to pillage the State's funds. These students cannot know that embezzlement can occur with the determining contribution of those who act as the Law's custodians who directly act to subvert "rights" into "wrongs."

Justice... justice...

CHAPTER 2

THE HUNCHBACKS THAT EMPTY THE STATE'S COFFERS

It was not difficult to find oneself in direct contrast with what was happening during the first turbulent years of the first monarchy. Italian Unification had led everyone to imagine a romantic future with a nation that was young and vigorous that was geared towards building a society of generalized wealth. This of course was all chatter. Just as one waking up from a dream, the country found itself having to deal with a ruling class that was unprepared and dishonest. They were arrogant and hungry for privileges. Damned Savoys!

The rich, by swindling and cheating, managed to accumulate a vast amount of wealth that made them even richer. In the meantime, the poor, despite not having any property to their names, found themselves burdened by taxes and they drowned in misery beyond the point of survival. The gap between social classes was vast.

Those in power, especially the King, had access to so many privileges that they are not even comparable to the ones available today despite their showiness because they all considered the State to be theirs. It was not necessary to steal: it was sufficient to merely take. Who would challenge them? The Savoys, all of them—the gentleman, the good man, the soldier, and the "tiny sabre"—had 14 million lira in appanage at their disposal.[18] This is as much as the King in Germany that guided Europe's engine, but more than the Queen of England. In proportion, they cost much more than what is sufficient to maintain the White House in Washington. They retrieved their annual checks without shame. In Rome, they lived in the Quirinale Palace that was the former residence of

---

[18] G. Bocca, *Il secolo sbagliato* (Milan, 1999).

the Pope with its 3,000 windows. In Castelporziano, they used a private beach and if they decided to stretch out their legs with a hunt, they could capture "310 pheasants, 69 boars, 2 deer, and a cat."[19] The people were dying of hunger? Well the administration of such a young government couldn't be everywhere just yet.

They were constantly too distracted by government matters to see the misery present on the city outskirts and the destitution present in the countryside. The needs of the people were the least of their problems because they were far removed from the court's interests.

King Umberto, who was charitable by nature, was often the first person present after a natural calamity occurred. He dispensed pats on the shoulders of the poor people who suffered in the cold and mud. He was also the first to flee the scene and forget about them quickly. He could not even suspect that the world might be divided into those who were wealthy and those who were poor. He believed that the real difference was in the fact that there were some people who knew how to ride a horse, with their back and shoulders straight and there were those who sat on the saddle like hunchbacks or sacks of potatoes. He possessed 1,300 horses scattered throughout Italy's cities. Every morning, even in rain or snow, he rode his horses, even for ten hour stretches.

There was no time to read. He considered the arts a great bore. He did not like intellectuals. When he was required to sign government documents, he shut himself in his room to fight with the papers while he stuck his tongue out of the side of his mouth as if to emphasize the effort that the bureaucracy was imposing him to make.

He considered politicians either fools or rascals and therefore he lumped them directly into the category of people who were unreliable and dangerous opportunists. He trusted the Marquis Rattazzi, for whom he waited every day at dusk behind the bushes so that he might hear

---

[19] P. Paulucci. *Alla corte di Re Umberto. Diario segreto* G. Calcagno, ed. (Milan, 1986).

about Crispi's latest hijinks.[20] When he had reached his heart's content after listening to the day's rumors, he returned to the palace and "when the King ascended the stairs, he would pass gas."[21] He did this before his trusted friend the Marquis Paolo Paulucci delle Roncole, who in turn wrote everything down in his diary, including the King's royal intestinal troubles. To the King's health!

Queen Margherita, in an age in which women were offered the privileges of having children and keeping quiet, had managed to earn for herself the right to express herself and offer criticism. To her, the men in her husband's government represented a "zoocracy"[22] whose members came in all shapes and sizes. Her son, Victor Emanuel III, upon reaching the throne, did not change his opinion regarding the moral value and trustworthiness of the Italian ruling class. The ministers he called before him to swear their loyalty belonged to the category of "nonentities."[23] What made them worse, in his eyes, was the fact that the only reason that they became involved at all in politics was for personal profit and therefore their actions and choices had one end: to fill their pockets.

Unfortunately, all of this was tragically true. With the excuse of administrating, they snatched up everything that they could get their hands on and that they were capable of physically carrying off.

The most prestigious recognition to which they could hope to aspire was to receive a public contract because it would allow them to earn beyond what was legitimate all while using construction material that was shoddy at best. Who cared if the buildings collapsed and workers died under the rubble?

They even speculated upon the monument erected to commemorate Victor Emanuel II that was to be erected upon the *Campidoglio*. They had held numerous public contests that had cost thousands of lira but the project had never gone beyond its cornerstone.

---

[20] Ibid.

[21] Ibid.

[22] G. Artieri, *Cronaca del Regno d'Italia: da Porta Pia all'intervento* (Milan, 1977).

[23] D. Mack Smith, *I Savoia re d'Italia* (Milan, 1989).

The historic Right, believing that they had "made" Italy, retained the right to govern it as though it were a building they owned. The Left, always historic, reached a position of power with quite an appetite and the scandals that saw it as the protagonist were murky and poorly hidden. The little good that they managed to accomplish quickly vanished. Many of the bad things they managed to accomplish are things that we are still trying to get rid of today.

Foreign observers did not have any trouble seeing such an unsustainable level of dishonesty in public life, but the practical consequences were irrelevant. If the news stories published abroad were particularly damaging, there were two possibilities: offer the journalists money so that they would soften their criticism in the future or expel those undesirable moralists. Thirty or so political commentators were on the Ministry of Internal Affairs' payroll while the *Corriere della Sera*, which politely but resolutely offered some level of criticism, found that its telephones were tapped.

There was less freedom in this so-called democratic Italy than in Austria under the authoritarian reign of the Habsburgs. Vilfredo Pareto and Maffeo Pantaleoni, to name two intellectuals, left the country and sought professorship, in Switzerland in order to teach whatever their conscience told them to be right.

All of the crooks and dishonest people, however, remained.

Giovanni Nicotera, the very powerful Minister of Internal Affairs, behaved as though he were a hero of the Risorgimento though he was quite infamous. He had participated in Pisacane's expedition but then proceeded to betray his chief and all of his friends without a second thought. He was the key witness in the trial of the "300 young and strong youths."[24] His bribery was the reason that they were all condemned. He was the

---

[24] *La Gazzetta d'Italia,* starting from November 2, 1878, published an investigative report that was destined to recount the truth concerning several anecdotes of the Risorgimento that, up until that point, had been presented in a commendatory fashion. Nicotera took legal action against the newspaper, editor, and journalist. The court, though it recognized the published data as truthful condemned them all "with a light sentence."

one who revealed their system of encryption that they used to communicate amongst themselves. He was also the man who named all of their accomplices who, up until that point, no one had known about. He declared that he had participated in the insurrection but "only to destroy the entire plan." It was for this reason that the Bourbon Court was grateful to him. But could he really become the man in charge of ensuring public order for the men who replaced the Bourbon monarchs?

Francesco Crispi withdrew money from the State's banks as if they were from his own personal bank account. He managed to subtract funds even from charitable projects such as the funds collected to help the victims of an earthquake in Calabria.

After the defeat in Adua, he left the position of Prime Minister and took several boxes of papers with him. These boxes included letters and telegrams, and other files that represented a part of the State's history. He brought these papers home as if they were his own. When Crispi died, several years later, the Italian State decided to purchase those documents (in reality, those documents were already property of the State) and paid Crispi's heirs to retrieve them.

Everyone scraped up what they could manage, though this worked out better from positions of authority. There were no legislative measures, particularly those of financial nature, that were not associated with some murky ulterior motives. An example? In 1903, the Minister of Finance called his home in Genoa. "Is that you, my dear?" It was. "Look," he warned, "tomorrow a law will be passed that will have an enormous impact on the stock market." Certain stocks, which were carefully detailed, were destined to lose several percentage points while others would have gained them and this could have caused them to profit a great deal. "Is this all clear?" "Perfectly!" But just to ensure that there was no doubt, he offered an even more explicit direction: "Tomorrow, you should sell the stocks that are in the first list and buy the largest number of stocks possible in the second list." It was pointless to be selfish. "Tell your father and our families so that they might all do the same." There was no time to lose, if not but to make one final comment: "How nice! I am so happy...."[25]

The Representative Rocco Zerbi, who was accused of illegally pocketing a half-million lira, was found dead.[26] Did he die of a heart attack or was it a suicide? Certainly Minister Rosano committed suicide when, taking advantage of the role he had in the government, he was able to ensure that his client was acquitted for a fee of 400,000 lira.[27] In those same years, an average worker worked for 10 hours to earn 3 lira. Since a position in Parliament was worth more than an insurance policy, Giuseppe Luciani managed to convince Pio Frezza to stab Raffaele Sonzogno so that he might succeed him as a candidate (with a very high probability of obtaining the position) in the fifth Roman district.[28] Having stolen the man's seat, he proceeded to steal the man's wife as well. The crime occurred on February 6, 1875, but was only discovered ten years later. Justice... justice...

They said, with some exaggeration, that that final decade of the nineteenth century represented the first economic miracle. In reality, the nature of production had a savage quality to it: it was based entirely on improvidence, a taste for adventure, and a strong desire to commit robbery by those who were strongest. The banks were the first to act as a terrible example because they behaved like usurers. They required interest rate requirements that were impossible to meet and that in fact actually made it impossible to actually obtain funds. The money went to those who already had money so that they might accumulate even more. They preferred to deal with speculators[29] rather than businessmen and preferred to help their friends rather than to ensure that the system functioned in a correct manner. The subsidies were planned in advance and the passage

---

[25] U. Guspini, *L'orecchio del regime* (Milan, 1973).
[26] Archivio storico della Camera dei deputati, parliamentary proceedings, first semester 1906.
[27] I. Montanelli, *L'Italia di Giolitti* (Milan, 1974).
[28] G. Artieri, *Cronaca del Regno d'Italia: da Porta Pia all'intervento* (Milan, 1977).
[29] I. Montanelli, *L'Italia di Giolitti*.

of the funds, from one party to the next, implicitly carried with it the right to retain a portion as though it were a sort of tax or fee for the passage. It seems as though one is reading the news from Lombardy and Tuscany today but these stories are all one hundred years old. The dates have changed but the substance has not. Even the mechanisms, though they have become a bit more sophisticated, have maintained their structures and developments intact.

The State did not intervene. What authority did it have anyway? It limited itself to exerting pressure towards favoring certain groups that suited its best interests. Rubattino became a wealthy man thanks to his Patriotic efforts and his shipping company. The railways of the State, which had been privatized, were repurchased by the State to help its owners amass a small fortune. Merchant shipping companies and the Navy became a market of illegal business and were built upon contracts that ensured shipments and supplies.

Admiral Bettolo was accused of showing "favoritism."[30] Carlo Mirabello, a high-ranking official with many decorations, and who was the "Provisory" Minister of War never quite had the opportunity to fight... neither by land nor by sea. He faced an epic battle in Parliament to ensure that his Ministry's financial accounts remained State secrets. This was the only way to ensure that many of his officials avoided jail. These officials had preferred bribes rather than military honor.

Anyone who stayed behind and watched risked to be considered a fool. Therefore, everyone sought to take advantage of his/her respective position. The Director of the Bank of Naples, in disguise as a priest, attempted to flee the country with 2.5 million euro dangling between his legs and from the inside of his tunic. The head of the Bank of Genoa, Enrico Baldini needed to send 6 million lira in cash to the central branch and kept 2.5 million.[31] He substituted the missing stacks with blocks of plywood so that the discovery would not be made too quickly. Angelo

---

[30] Two parliament investigations, concluded in 1906 and 1908 that came to a close under severe criticism.

[31] G. Artieri, *Cronaca del Regno d'Italia: da Porta Pia all'intervento* (Milan, 1977).

Sommaruga robbed thousands of people when he told them to purchase stocks that were barely worth the paper they were printed on.[32] These could be considered the ancestors of today's junk bonds and were capable of making several holding companies wealthy while emptying the wallets of tens of millions of people.

Emanuele Notarbartolo, on the other hand, lost his life. He had noticed that there were many anomalies surrounding the Bank of Sicily so he reported them. He was killed while on a train. The evidence allowed for a representative, Palizzolo, to be called before the court. He had discovered a very simple and infallible way to make money. He gambled the bank's money on the stock market. If he won, he went to the teller to retrieve his profits, which resulted that he had personally earned. If he lost, it was not a problem. The institution's investments had not gone well. The network of accomplices revealed itself to be too complex. He was acquitted.[33]

The same protagonists of these episodes confessed that the "illness" was in a critical state but that there was no cure. Giovanni Giolitti, the tall man who always wore black to frighten the superstitious Neapolitans, found a splendid way to justify his behavior: "The tailor that must sew a suit for a hunchback must cut the fabric so that it forms a hump." It was not his fault that people were that way. He, who was a rigorous Jansenist in his personal life, had no scruples in his management of power and was not ashamed of his shamelessness. When he left his position of power, the "crippled" had multiplied and that hunchback seemed to walk in an even more crooked fashion.

---

[32] Anonymous, *Giudicatemi* (Milan, 1885). The text offered a detailed report of the trial that took place before the correctional court of Rome from August 31 to September 18, 1885. In the appendix, one can find the closing statements made by the public prosecutor as well as those of the defendant's lawyers: Coboevich, Vitale, and Panettoni.

[33] E. Magrì, "Milano, 1899: la mafia debutta in tribunal" in *Il Giornale*, November 13, 1999.

It seemed as though the entire country could get used to the worst case scenario. Scandals were becoming the norm and rebellions were rare. A tailor named Giorgianni climbed up to the Parliament's gallery and proceeded to throw rocks and nails upon the representatives.[34]

In any case, the King's magistrates remained conveniently quiet. Justice… justice…

---

[34] A result of the parliamentary proceedings of July 25, 1880.

CHAPTER 3

WHOM SHOULD WE BLAME
FOR OUR LACK OF TRUST IN POLITICIANS?

The magistrates who write books may be right. Sure, the Parliament is strangled between delays and obstacles... ok, the personnel may be sparse... let us also throw in the budgets that have been cut....

But if Italy's justice system places near the bottom of the international ranking system, whose fault is it?

The desks of many are covered with files that are avoided or handled slowly and inconsistently. Others seem like they have little to do. There should be 58 military judges but there are only 48 because 10 also hold other roles. In 2011, there were 208 first-level sentences issued (in other words approximately 60, one and a half per week for each of the 3 courts).[35] Out of those instances, 113 appealed the sentences and 40 of those cases reached the Supreme Court. After military duty was no longer obligatory, only minor issues that most often regarded disciplinary measures were addressed. According to a suggestive image offered by Vito Nicolò Diana, the President of the Supreme Court: "This is like having a Ferrari circling around a courtyard."[36] Who must intervene so that we might have jobs distributed in a convenient manner?

---

[35] They have an office in Rome at Palazzo Cesi; in Naples in the former convent of Santa Maria degli Angeli di Pizzofalcone; in Verona, at Palazzo Santa Lucia. In Rome they also have the Court of Appeals and the Office of the Public Prosecutor; the Military Surveillance Court and the Public Prosecutor's Office at the Court of Cassation.

[36] Speech at the opening of the 2010 judiciary year.

If the Italian magistrates inspire little trust in the European community, and much less at home, how would it be possible to compile a list of the accused, where nearly all are under fire, except themselves?

Several politicians have sacrificed everything for their profession. Sometimes it has even cost them their lives and they have been acknowledged only posthumously for their efforts. These acknowledgements are often not even adequate in comparison to their sacrifice. However, just as there were those who made the ultimate sacrifice, there are those who strayed and became associated with organized crime, the enemy: Giancarlo Giusti[37] and Vincenzo Giglio.[38]

The Italian judicial system knows both the pinnacles of professional excellence, but there are also a few inevitable rotten apples. But besides the best of the best and the worst of the worst, don't those people who represent the "normalcy" of the system have anything to say for themselves?

In the meantime, it is the magistrates who have accepted that politics make its triumphant entrance in the courts and attorney offices, with both parties being respectively represented.

Each political party has managed to gain the support of its own "group" of judges, a few of which have managed to obtain significant political roles. To offer an example: Oscar Luigi Scalfaro, who sustained that he had the judge's "gown sewn onto his skin," though he was unable to practice his craft for very long, ascended the steps to the Quirinale Palace which opened the door for him to the Presidency of the Republic.

This sort of spoils system has wound up damaging the primary value of the magistracy: autonomy. The law purists prefer to refer to this as

---

[37] L. Ferrarella, "Il giudice, la promozione, e le escort: quel caso che imbarazza il Csm" in *Corriere della Sera*, March 29, 2012. The judge was arrested on March 28, 2012 after being accused of accepting bribes in the form of trips and prostitutes paid by an *'ndrangheta* boss.

[38] L. Ferrarella, "Il giudice anti 'ndrangheta che rivelava tutti i segreti al boss. Condannato insieme a un consigliere comunale calabrese" in *Corriere della Sera*, February 7, 2013.

their "tertiary" or "third-party" quality. During a trial, a judge cannot side with either the plaintiff or the defendant, but rather the judge chooses to side with the "third-party": the law.

That this impartial attitude might become more solid is not enough, however. It is much more important that the sentence appears to be free from bias from the outside. Otherwise, every decision, though it might be made consciously and in a serene manner, will always be subject to criticism for bias that may have been hidden or latent.

The "branding" of a party compromises the future of a magistrate that, after a brief foray in politics, returns to his former activity. It also compromises his past activity because the public opinion is authorized to believe that any investigation may not have been carried out in a completely impartial fashion. We are even encouraged to think that such investigations may have been carefully devised to conquer a certain measure of visibility in order to back political adversaries into a corner.

Some believe that "a certain amount of time must pass between a scandalous investigation and a candidature."[39] But nearly everyone accepts the notion that a magistrate, after a political career, "cannot carry out a role in the legal field."[40] Yet simple directions such as this cannot become imperatives.

When Nitto Francesco Palma was Minister of Justice, he had presented a bill that would offer some more rigidity regarding a magistrate's entrance into the political sphere and their respective exit. The proposal was accepted by Senator Felice Casson and seemed inspired by common sense rather than by the thought of garnering any recognition. Politicians could not become candidates in places where they exercised their judicial power in order to avoid what would be considered a "conflict of interest."

---

[39] M. Rebotti, "Dambruoso al Corriere. Magistrati In politica. Una volta candidati non tornino indietro" in *Corriere della Sera*, February 6, 2013.
[40] M. Martinelli, "I pm rispettino le competenze. Vietti: «Emergono speculazioni spericolate ma bisogna evitare iniziative estemporanee». Il Parlamento potrebbe introdurre nuove norme sul problema dei magistrati che entrano in politica" in *Corriere della Sera*, February 4, 2013.

After their political careers, they would need to be relocated as part of the government's legal service. Palma and Casson had both been magistrates, though one was a member of the PDL party and the other a member of the PD. Their professionalism and their different ideologies should have been enough to ensure the success of their initiative. In reality, the bill they had drafted floated in the government for a while before it inevitably sank. Nitto Palma commented: "I am not certain as to what the reasons were for blocking this bill. Certainly there was opposition on the part of the magistrates. Even the State's lawyers fought until the bitter end because they feared that they would be surrounded by magistrates in high ranking positions with seniority."[41]

The magistracy's political nature does not only manifest itself through explicit candidacies on electoral lists. The elections to the Magistracy and to the Association of Magistrates' Superior Council (which are, respectively, the only system's entity of self-regulation and the other is the union) occur through the presentation of lists of candidates whose ideologies are explicitly written. Then there are the signatures on proclamations... program manifestos to share... demonstrations to which they must participate... public declarations and political stances taken...

The magistrates sustain that they have the same rights as any other citizen and that therefore they are free to associate themselves with whomever they please, state their opinions, declare their political preferences, and actively participate in elections. It goes without saying that one cannot prevent a judge or a public prosecutor from embarking upon a political career or choosing to end one. One cannot prevent a soccer referee from keeping silent on his being a fan of a certain team either. However, if a referee declares that he is a fan of a given team, he hangs up his whistle and ends his professional career.

The "third-party" cannot become a "party" but once it is a "party" it is a "party" forever.

---

[41] D. Martirano, "Intervista a Nitto Palma. 'Toghe in politica? Sia una scelta senza ritorno'" in *Corriere della Sera*, February 2, 2013.

Nevertheless, even the judges who have not been lured by the prospect of a political career are not exactly known for their efficiency and speed. Our justice system advances with the speed of a snail: with hesitant slowness.

Statistics say that the average Italian couple's divorce takes 800 days to be finalized. In order to receive money owed, 1,210 are needed. On average, 10 years are required to finalize a bankruptcy and 9 years are required before a case is taken to trial at the tax and revenue court, though every once in a while, it actually may take longer. Germano Grassivaro waited 19 years to receive the revision of a ranking that would have allowed him to win a contest. In the meantime, he reached the age of retirement. He was a professor at the University of Venice and Padua and aspired to become the Scientific Expert for the embassy in Buenos Aires. "We are sorry" was the response he received. Even though his resumè was appreciated and he demonstrated convincing professional qualities, the committee chose differently.

It was the spring of 1993. In the age of politics, it was the equivalent of the Jurassic Era. Bill Clinton met Boris Yeltsin for the first time. Berlusconi was only a building magnate and the owner of the Mediaset network.

Grassivaro turned to the law. Only on December 5, 2011 did he receive the verdict: another man went to Argentina in his place but the position was technically his.[42] "I will ask for damages." There was work to be done for the lawyers.

There are 240,000 lawyers and the tariffs reward those who sign more acts and not those who shorten the trial times. Piercamillo Davigo, who during the *Mani Pulite* investigation had earned himself the nickname "dottor Sottile" (Doctor Subtle), has revealed that in France there are 7.1 lawyers for each judge. In Italy, there are 26.4 lawyers for each judge. There is something wrong about this proportion.

---

[42] G.A. Stella, "Se la diplomazia va a rilento. Vince il concorso 19 anni dopo. La domanda nel '93. 'Sono in pensione, ora chiedo i danni'" in *Corriere della Sera*, March 31, 2012.

In 2011, there were 2,369 cases of unjust imprisonment. This puts Italy in last place in all of Europe for the fifth consecutive year. The State paid 46 million euro for these judicial errors.[43] Why should the State pay, and not the judge who committed the error? Yet the Italians, in one of the few referenda that actually reached a quorum, expressed their opinions out of their own personal "responsibility" as citizens. It is strange that the defenders of the Constitution and the valorous supporters of the theory that the citizens need to be protagonists of political decisions actually do not operate to ensure that the will of those citizens is carried out. In the courts and in the attorneys' offices they sustained the belief that a judge who risks personally paying for his mistakes loses his serenity. Well sure! Even when an accountant prepares a company's accounting, a doctor enters an operating room, or an engineer signs his calculations for the required amount of armored cement to support a bridge he or she is taking a risk! But when any of these professionals commits an error in their line of work, a judge conducts an investigation and often the professional is sent to trial for making an error in their profession. Why should a judge receive such different and privileged treatment?

With a proposal, the Minister of Justice Paola Severino had imagined a sort of "indirect" responsibility. The State would have paid for the damage and would have then turned to the judge or public prosecutor to pay "not less than half of their annual salary."[44] There was no time to discuss and approve this measure either.

Obviously the possibility of having to personally pay for something reduces the serenity necessary to pass any sort of judgment. But doesn't the absence of serenity risk rendering the legal process presumptuous, in virtue of the fact that it cannot itself be judged?

---

[43] S. Zurlo, "Spesi 84 milioni per fascicoli scaduti. Migliaia di casi l'anno in prescrizione: ma lo Stato paga lo stesso. E per recuperare un credito servono 1200 giorni" in *Il Giornale*, April 1, 2012.
[44] M. Stanganelli, "Responsabilità dei magistrati: il Governo «sì, ma indiretta». Severino media, lo Stato potrà rivalersi del 50 per cento sul giudice" in *Il Messaggero*, June 6, 2012.

Statistics say that 42% of detainees are held in temporary custody. This means that nearly 1 out of every 2 detainees are awaiting trial. Are all of these people so dangerous that they have to await trial behind bars? How many of those detainees were found to be innocent and therefore carried out a preventative sentence that was imposed upon them?

The numbers are quite frightening, yet they do not tell the whole story. Behind each statistic that the bureaucracy files with arithmetic petulance, there is a human being with a story. Most of the time, that story is a dramatic one. For the "system," each error is a percentage point on a chart but those who find themselves on the other side of that chart, in jail and innocent, feels their life slipping out of their fingers.

The committees, such as that of Grosso, Nordio, and Pisapia, release numerous tomes that preach the decriminalization of certain crimes but then these studies are forgotten in some drawer. There is a need to simplify the legal code but, on the contrary, each time they see to find the way to complicate it with brand new crimes. Most of the time, these crimes are actually old ones characterized by new wording.

The result is that every year, the period of prescription expires for 165,000 files. This means that the 84 million euro that have been spent for paper and for investigations have been completely wasted.[45]

The sword of justice is made of tin. If one has valid motives that need to be defended they should be able to rely on a system like that of England, where in many cases executive sentences are issued in a few days, though in more complex cases this may take at most a few months. If, however, one is at fault, there is no better system in which to find oneself than the Italian justice system. Its murky yet meticulous character winds upon itself until the period of prescription expires. The responsibility of those at fault extinguishes itself as though nothing happened. The only thing that the victims are left with is the rage for a compensation that they will never receive.

---

[45] S. Zurlo, "Spesi 84 milioni per fascicoli scaduti."

These delays leave open the gates of jails even for serious delinquents, who are often unpunished.

It is not rare to see that due to the expiration of a given period of prescription a dangerous criminal may be set free. Such is the case of Mauro "Nico" Marra, which caused controversy and scandal. He was a hired killer who worked for the *camorra* boss Raffaele Cutolo. In the 1980s, he participated in 80 ambushes and it seems that he killed 30 people. He repented and was condemned to serve a twenty-year sentence. This sentence was annulled by the Supreme Court, and a new trial was ordered but the proceedings were never instituted. So now this man is free.[46]

Perhaps the notion of "obligatory legal action" should be eliminated or at least revisited with common sense. Each crime must be prosecuted... ok.... Sooner or later we will need to instate a hierarchy of tasks. Some must come first while others must come later. Some need not be addressed at all.

I personally recall the "Years of Lead" when Turin was able to drag certain members of the *Brigate Rosse* and *Prima Linea* to court. During the trials, it was not a rare occurrence for one of the accused to insult one of the judges. The public prosecutor would proceed to request the written records of the trial in order to hold the accused in contempt of court. They then proceeded to call for a separate trial that often overlapped two or three times with the Supreme Court's trial. It then became necessary to transfer those terrorists from their maximum security prisons to the court with massive police escorts. In the end, people who already were to carry out 2 or 3 life sentences apiece (which none of them actually carried to full term anyway) received an extra 20 days of prison. Wasn't this a waste of energy, money, and professional skills?

Upon analyzing various cases throughout Italy's courts and public prosecutor's offices there are too many trials that appear "strange" and too many sentences that leave one in a state of stupor.

---

[46] R.R., "Giustizia lumaca, libero il killer. Scarcerato per scadenza termini un pluriomicida della Nco di Cutolo" in *Roma*, January 9, 2013.

A college of judges condemned the scientists of the Committee for Great Risks for involuntary manslaughter for not having predicted the 2009 earthquake in L'Aquila. In the motivations, it is obviously written that the scientists were not condemned for not having read the future. The document states: "That which the accused are condemned for is not, *a posteriori*, the missing prediction of the earthquake or failing to evacuate the city." A bit further, the document states: "They are condemned for being in violation of specific obligations regarding evaluation, prediction, and prevention of the seismic risk."

What were those scientists supposed to have done? They should have warned everyone about the risk in an exaggerated manner so that they would have been spared not from the earthquake, but from a judicial system that states essentially they were not condemned for "not predicting" the earthquake, but that they were condemned for "not predicting" the earthquake. These are things that happen... only in Italy though.[47]

On December 21, 2000, a bank teller was fired because he approved a loan for himself and proceeded to take money from the bank's funds. The judge from the Milan Court gave him back his job because it "took into consideration the physical depression to which he had been subjected." Another worker lost his job for a fraud that he conducted against his own place of work. The judge annulled any disciplinary action "in order to carefully consider the complexity of the investigation in order to ascertain the crime." From a civil liberty's standpoint this action is just. The only problem is that, over time, the investigation proved that the fraudulent activity did occur but he kept his job because "in the meantime, the accused behaved in an exemplary manner and therefore offered proof that his case needed to be revisited" according to the Court of Messina. In Bergamo, a worker started a fight with one of his colleagues and was not fired due to a court decision: "The sanctions must be given in proportion to the gravity of the crime." Another worker had submitted a

---

[47] P. Battista, "Sentenze rischiose come terremoti" in *Corriere della Sera*, January 21, 2013.

medical certificate and his boss soon found himself contesting the head of the CISL (workers' labor union) Raffaele Bonanni in front of a television crew. The employer had retained that the fiduciary relationship between him and his worker had been broken but the judge had a different opinion. The reason the employee was absent was because he had an illness that prevented him from "carrying out repetitive strains during his eight-hour work day" (as quoted from the proceedings' records of the Court of Turin). He could handle strains outside of those hours, however.

The judges also pardoned a *carabiniere* who stole money as well. He had stolen 80 euro and was discharged but readmitted by the magistrate. "It does not appear reasonable to inflict the maximum penalty and taking into consideration the multiple circumstances that would have advised a more careful consideration of his career merits, all well-deserved, his young age, and his inexperience at the moment of the crime (it was his first year in service) in addition to the simple nature of the crime." Effectively, 80 euro is not a vast amount....[48]

Even a judge, Luigi Passanis, who was accused of first degree "corruption of legal counsel," retained his position.[49]

---

[48] P. Sapegno, "Il carabiniere che rubava perdonato dai giudici. Cacciato dopo il furto di 80 euro, il Tar lo reintegra: «è giovane e inesperto»" in *La Stampa*, June 17, 2012.

[49] G. Salvaggiulo, "Condannato per corruzione il giudice resta al suo post. 'Sentenza venduta,' nei guai il president del Tar Marche" in *La Stampa*, October 14, 2012. The article recounts the version of the attorney who supports the plaintiff's side. According to the investigation, when the colleague was in Calabria, he had favored a certain businessman, a former representative for the Forza Italia party. The trial concluded with a sentence of three years and six months (though the public prosecutor had requested six years). The judge in question, in the meantime, had been transferred to the Regional Administrative Court of the Marche region. He claimed to be innocent and filed an appeal so that he could continue to carry out his work. The PD party presented a parliamentary interrogation to invoke his "resignation or at least his suspension" and to call for disciplinary action "for the great damage inflicted upon the magistrate's prestige and credibility."

Meanwhile, Mario Conte, a judge in the Court of Bergamo, was accused of drug trafficking. He waited for 15 years before he was acquitted and returned to his position. Did he offer any comments? "I risked death."[50]

In Viterbo, a trial went on for 4 years, involving a preliminary hearing judge along with 5 Supreme Court judges. The defendant was a deaf-mute who was accused of verbal abuse. His neighbor had dragged him to court because she felt mocked by his "grumbling."[51]

Even verdicts can conflict with one another. The use of the word *puttana*[52] can account for a conviction even if the insult is hurled at someone who is truly in the profession. However, one can legally call one's husband "a criminal assassin" even if he has never actually murdered anyone.[53]

If one shouts "buffoon" to Berlusconi it is ok, but he cannot be called a "cretin," such as was the case of a few municipal council members. The word "cretin" "implies a degrading concept of political power."[54] The word *azzeccagarbugli*[55] referred to a mayor is grounds for a trial while a professor accusing the university president of being "a liar and cheat" can stand "as long as it was said while the person was carrying out their labor-sanctioned duties."[56]

For the Regional Administrative Court the use of the word *frocio*[57] is not a crime, but for the Supreme Court, it is. The classical Italian phrase

---

[50] L. Fazzo, "'Io pm ascolto dopo 15 anni ho anche rischiato di morire'. Il giudice Conte racconta il suo calvario nei tribunali iniziato nel '97. Accusato dai colleghi di traffici di droga e armi, si ammalò gravemente. Ora è prosciolto con formula piena" in *Il Giornale*, July 20, 2012.

[51] R.L., "Il sordomuto a processo per ingiurie" in *Libero*, April 22, 2012.

[52] *Translator's note*: "whore."

[53] M. Zucchetti, "Se il bon ton lo decidono i giudici. 'Frocio', 'buffone' o 'cretino': la giustizia dibatte per anni su ogni tipo d'insulto" in *Il Giornale*, August 2, 2012.

[54] Ibid.

[55] *Translator's note*: a shyster, or someone who employs unethical means to carry out their job.

[56] Ibid.

[57] *Translator's note*: "faggot."

"you don't know who I am" can take you straight to court "because it intimidates and limits one's psychological freedom." The promise to "flunk" someone, coming from a teacher to a student, receives the same treatment because "it inculcates a strong sense of fear that damages the student's moral freedom."[58]

The courts are filled with such cases. After many years of litigation, it was possible to establish that it is legal to shake the crumbs off of one's tablecloth from one's balcony but a noisy air conditioning unit is cause for a conviction. Urinating in public is a crime "even if the genitals are not visible or if the urination takes place in the shadows."[59]

The issues become more complex when one enters the realm of the workplace. Telling one's superior that they are "crazy" is allowed because it is considered "constructive criticism." An employee is also allowed to tell one's boss to "go to hell" because "it does not compromise the employee's fiduciary relationship with the company." If, however, an employer decides to tell an employee that they are a "nuisance" or that they "do not understand anything" that employer is liable "in virtue of the expressive content."[60]

Don Gianni Antoniazzi, from Carpenedo di Venezia, had to pay a fine of 1,282 euro for "ringing the church bells in a manner that was not in accordance with the law." Another priest, Francesco Tondello who was the parish priest for the Church of San Paolo Apostolo in Padua, was sentenced to install sound-absorbing panels around the chapel because an accountant who lived next door was disturbed by the noise.[61]

In compensation, Italy's great mysteries remain enshrouded by a cloak of question marks. The Court of Assizes and Appeals of Brescia acquitted the neo-Fascists Carlo Maria Maggi, Delfo Zorzi, Maurizio Tramonte, and General Francesco Delfino from the accusation of being

---

[58] Ibid.

[59] Ibid.

[60] Ibid.

[61] F. Caccia, "Se un giudice ordina il silenziatore all'oratorio. Obbligo di pannelli fonoassorbenti. Il prete: chiudo" in *Corriere della Sera*, May 5, 2012.

the authors of the Brescia Massacre that occurred on May 28, 1974. It took them nearly 40 years to "not know" who set off those bombs and why.[62] This is similar to the question marks still in place regarding the Piazza Fontana Massacre.

On the other hand, there are far too many truths known regarding the Ustica disaster that occurred on June 27, 1980. The deaths of 81 people resulted when an Alitalia DC-9 airplane crashed en route from Bologna to Palermo. The highest Italian criminal court supported the hypothesis that the explosion was caused by a bomb[63] that was located aboard the plane. The Italian civil court called for the compensation of certain family members of certain victims that were struck by a missile.[64]

Our judicial system is slow, contorted, contradictory, and ultimately unjust. Justice... justice...

---

[62] M. Cervi, "Brescia, se questa è giustizia. È la mostruosa lentezza della legge ad aver ucciso la verità in piazza della Loggia" in *Il Giornale*, June 15, 2012.

[63] Sentence 3407 pronounced by the first section of the Penal section of the Court of Cassation on March 2, 2007. The hypothesis on the causes of the disaster was formulated in the context of a trial held for "misdirection" and several officials were forced to answer to these accusations.

[64] Sentence 1871 pronounced by the third section of the Civil section of the Court of Cassation on January 28, 2013.

INDEX OF NAMES

Mack Smith, Denis, 6, 8, 79, 156-157, 198,
MacLaine, Shirley, 71
Maggi, Carlo Maria, 216
Magrì, Enzo, 139, 203
Magris, Claudio, 154
Malaparte, Curzio, 177
Mancino, Nicola, 35, 72
Mannelli, Giambattista, 129-130
Manzoni, Alessandro, 152
Marchesi, Concetto, 172
Margherita of Savoy, Queen, 135, 198
Marini, Franco, 72
Marra, Mauro "Nico," 212
Martinati, Antonio, 193
Martinelli, M., 207
Martini, Ferdinando, 138
Martirano, Dino, 208
Martucci, Roberto, 81-82, 116
Massidda, Piergiorgio, 65
Mathiez, Albert, 20
Mauro, Ezio, 30
Mazzini, Giuseppe, 59, 97-98, 101, 106, 116, 135, 156
Mazzonis, Filippo, 132-133
Medici, Ferdinando de', 32
Mele, Cosimo, 68
Melloni, Mario, 153
Menabrea, Luigi Federico, 128, 183, 188
Mieli, Paolo, 158-159
Miglioli, Guido, 165
Mirabello, Carlo, 202
Momigliano, Attilio, 176
Momigliano, Eucardio, 164

Montanelli, Indro, 32, 83, 161, 201
Monti, Augusto, 164
Monti, Mario, 30, 40, 57, 92
Montmasson, Rosalie, 144-145
Mordini, Antonio, 108, 119, 184
Munchau, Wolfgang, 92
Muscetta, Carlo, 117
Musolino, Benedetto, 109
Mussolini, Benito, 7, 38, 144, 159-173, 175, 177, 179

Nani, Giorgia, 42-43
Napolitano, Giorgio, 7, 30, 34-36
Narducci, Alessandro, 138
Natale, G., 138
Nenni, Pietro, 164
Nesti, Gustavo, 167
Nicoletta, Antonio, 6
Nicotera, Giovanni, 139, 199
Nievo, Ippolito, 82, 116, 118
Nievo, Stanislao, 83
Nitti, Francesco Saverio, 83-84
Notarbartolo, Emanuele, 203

Ostellino, Piero, 93

Pace, Alessandro, 36
Pais Serra, Francesco, 138
Pajetta, Giancarlo, 175-176
Pallavicini Trivulzio, Giorgio, 123
Palma, Nitto Francesco, 207-208
Pancrazi, Claudio, 139
Pantaleoni, Maffeo, 137, 199

ABOUT THE AUTHOR

LORENZO DEL BOCA, journalist, was the president of the Federazione Nazionale della Stampa Italiana (National Federation of the Italian Press) from 1996 to 2001, and the president of the Consiglio nazionale dell'Ordine dei Giornalisti (National Counsel of the Association of Journalists) from 2001 to 2010. While reporting for *La Stampa* between 1980-2000, Del Boca's work followed prominent investigations and issues such as terrorism and events leading to the disbandment of mafia clans in northern Italy. His historical works are defined as "revisionist" because they stray away from traditional academic clichés. His interests focus on the Renaissance period and world war: *Maledetti Savoia, Indietro Savoia, Risorgimento disonorato, Polentoni* (available also in English, published by Bordighera Press and ILICA), *Italia bugiarda, Grande Guerra, piccoli generali.* Since 2012, Del Boca has been the director of the sacred representations of Good Friday in Romagnano, the town in which he lives and works.

SAGGISTICA

Taking its name from the Italian, which means essays, essay writing, or nonfiction, *Saggisitca* is a referred book series dedicated to the study of all topics and cultural productions that fall under what we might consider that larger umbrella of all things Italian and Italian/American.

Vito Zagarrio
The "Un-Happy Ending": Re-viewing The Cinema of Frank Capra. 2011. ISBN 978-1-59954-005-4. Volume 1.
Paolo A. Giordano, Editor
The Hyphenate Writer and The Legacy of Exile. 2010. ISBN 978-1-59954-007-8. Volume 2.
Dennis Barone
America / Trattabili. 2011. ISBN 978-1-59954-018-4. Volume 3.
Fred L. Gardaphè
The Art of Reading Italian Americana. 2011. ISBN 978-1-59954-019-1. Volume 4.
Anthony Julian Tamburri
Re-viewing Italian Americana: Generalities and Specificities on Cinema. 2011. ISBN 978-1-59954-020-7. Volume 5.
Sheryl Lynn Postman
An Italian Writer's Journey through American Realities: Giose Rimanelli's English Novels. "The most tormented decade of America: the 60s" ISBN 978-1-59954-034-4. Volume 6.
Luigi Fontanella
Migrating Words: Italian Writers in the United States. 2012. ISBN 978-1-59954-041-2. Volume 7.
Peter Covino & Dennis Barone, Editors
Essays on Italian American Literature and Culture. 2012. ISBN 978-1-59954-035-1. Volume 8.
Gianfranco Viesti
Italy at the Crossroads. 2012. ISBN 978-1-59954-071-9. Volume 9.
Peter Carravetta, Editor
Discourse Boundary Creation (Logos Topos Poiesis): A Festschrift in Honor of Paolo Valesio. ISBN 978-1-59954-036-8. Volume 10.
Antonio Vitti and Anthony Julian Tamburri, Editors
Europe, Italy, and the Mediterranean. ISBN 978-1-59954-073-3. Volume 11.
Vincenzo Scotti
Pax Mafiosa or War: Twenty Years after the Palermo Massacres. 2012. ISBN 978-1-59954-074-0. Volume 12.

Anthony Julian Tamburri, Editor
   Meditations on Identity. Meditazioni su identità. ISBN 978-1-59954-082-
   5. Volume 13.
Peter Carravetta, Editor
   *Theater of the Mind, Stage of History. A Festschrift in Honor of Mario
   Mignone.* ISBN 978-1-59954-083-2. Volume 14.

CPSIA information can be obtained at www.ICGtesting.com
Printed in the USA
BVOW03s1203150914

366681BV00005B/6/P